THE ULTIMATE
FROZEN
COCKTAILS & SMOOTHIES
ENCYCLOPEDIA

THE ULTIMATE
FROZEN
COCKTAILS & SMOOTHIES
ENCYCLOPEDIA

WALTER BURNS

Thunder Bay
P·R·E·S·S

SAN DIEGO

C O N

Warning
To avoid the risk of salmonella, use pasteurized eggs. The pasteurization process kills any harmful bacteria in the egg.

Thunder Bay Press
An imprint of Printers Row Publishing Group
10350 Barnes Canyon Road, Suite 100
San Diego, CA 92121
www.thunderbaybooks.com

All notations of errors or omissions should be addressed to Thunder Bay Press, Editorial Department, at the above address. All other correspondence (author inquiries, permissions) concerning the content of this book should be addressed to Moseley Road, Inc., 129 Main St., Suite B, Irvington, NY 10533.

Moseley Road Inc, www.moseleyroad.com
Publisher: Sean Moore
General Manager: Karen Prince
Editorial Director: Damien Moore
Production Director: Adam Moore
Project Editor and Art Director: Lisa Purcell Editorial & Design
Cover Design: Duncan Youel, www.oiloften.co.uk

Thunder Bay Press
Publisher: Peter Norton
Publishing Team: Lori Asbury, Ana Parker, Laura Vignale
Editorial Team: JoAnn Padgett, Melinda Allman, Traci Douglas
Production Team: Blake Mitchum, Rusty von Dyl

Library of Congress Cataloging-in-Publication Data:
Ultimate frozen cocktails and smoothies.
 pages cm
Includes bibliographical references and index.
ISBN 978-1-62686-434-4 (hardcover : alk. paper)
1. Cocktails. 2. Smoothies (Beverages)
TX951.U455 2015
641.87'4--dc23

Printed in China

19 18 17 16 15 1 2 3 4 5

T E N T S

C O N T E

N T S

A THIRST FOR ICE

In the late 1800s, around the time of the Spanish-American War, an American engineer in Cuba combined white rum, sugar, and lime juice over cracked ice and named the resulting drink after a nearby beach: Daiquiri. The recipe wasn't exactly new; by then British sailors had been drinking navy grog—a blend of rum, water, lime juice, and sugar—for more than a hundred years to ward off scurvy on long voyages. Their concoction was responsible for the epithet "limey." But shortly after the turn of the twentieth century the daiquiri had found its way to American bars, and it has been a perennial favorite ever since. Ernest Hemingway even had his name attached to one variation of the drink, cementing its appeal.

The story wasn't over yet, however. At some point in the 1930s, a bartender at El Floridita, one of Hemingway's favorite bars in Havana, stopped straining daiquiris and instead incorporated crushed ice into his version for an even colder, more bracing drink. With the advent of the electric blender, the frozen daiquiri became a phenomenon.

The original drink conformed to a classic cocktail formula—"one of sour, two of sweet, three of strong, four of weak"—so it lent itself to any number of variations involving fruit of all kinds. The strawberry, banana, and pineapple daiquiri—among many others—soon emerged. For some cocktail aficionados, these were just corruptions of the sacrosanct original. In reality, they were new developments in the long relationship between ice and cocktails.

DAWN OF THE ICE AGE

Cocktails weren't always iced. If we follow the word *cocktail* as far back as we can, the trail leads to late eighteenth-century London, where inns and public houses served weary travelers and gregarious locals an array of punches, toddies, and fizzes. Often, given the English climate, those drinks were served warm. But the American climate, with an inclination toward extreme heat and cold, gave rise to a much more expansive vision of the cocktail—one that helped define a distinctly American thirst for icy beverages.

The United States is the homeland of cocktail culture. Although we may entertain glamorous visions of such legendary European watering holes as the Savoy in London and Harry's American Bar in Paris, those establishments were actually the beneficiaries of Prohibition, which largely shut down what had been a scintillating American cocktail scene. Like the daiquiri, many of the classic drinks were invented in the nineteenth and early twentieth centuries, when circumstances combined to create an explosion of mixological creativity.

One reason for America's preeminence is its long love affair with two prime bases for cocktails: rum, which was a welcome by-product of the sugar trade, and American whiskies, especially rye and bourbon. After the War of 1812, when spirits were no longer taxed, and then 1832, when liquor licenses were extended to establishments that did not rent rooms, tinkering with mixed drinks became something of a national pastime. Spirits of all kinds, fresh fruits and juices, bitters (alcoholic beverages infused with herbal extracts), and other ingredients were combined in myriad ways to create everything from slings to juleps to martinis.

This exuberant cocktail culture was unique in more ways than one. Not only was there a democratic spirit to the very idea of an open bar, drinking establishments became arenas for all sorts of mingling, discussion, and debate. There was also something of a celebrity culture as well, in which top-tier "barmen" commanded starry-eyed adulation. Some of them, like Jerry Thomas and Harry Johnson, wrote encyclopedic manuals on how to mix drinks—books to which many contemporary bartenders have returned for inspiration.

Ice, however, didn't enter the picture in a significant way until the mid-nineteenth century. In 1806, a wealthy young Bostonian named Frederic Tudor had hatched a plan for harvesting ice from New England ponds and shipping it to heat-oppressed colonists in the West Indies. The difficulties were twofold: first, keeping his investment from literally melting away; second, convincing people that they should go out of their way to get ice for their drinks. After a string of false starts that nearly landed him in debtor's prison, Tudor started to win customers by offering free samples, occasionally encouraging local bars to offer the same drink with and without ice to see which version patrons preferred. As one might imagine, the idea of an icy cold sling or toddy quickly caught on, especially in such sweltering southern cities as Charleston and Atlanta.

Eventually, Tudor and his team worked out how to harvest, load, and insulate their ice efficiently for shipping. In 1833, Tudor even managed to ship more than 150 tons of it from Boston to Calcutta, supplying the ice for the gin and tonics of thousands of Anglo-Indian drinkers. Supplying India with ice would eventually make Tudor nearly a quarter of a million dollars—a staggering sum in those days. Meanwhile, the domestic ice industry would boom. Within 20 years of that shipment to Calcutta, tens of thousands of tons of ice were traveling annually by rail to dozens of U.S. cities. Availability could hardly keep pace with demand, and, by mid-century, New England in particular teemed with new ice shippers and vendors. It was something of an Ice Rush, and Frederic Tudor was known as the "Ice King."

The Civil War did little to stem the growth of the ice industry—or the cocktail scene. In fact, it was in 1862, in the midst of the conflict, that Jerry Thomas wrote *The Bon Vivant's Companion or How to Mix Drinks,* also known as *The Bartender's Guide.* The first book on mixology published in America, Thomas's tome evolved in subsequent editions as his extraordinary career unfolded; it was to American cocktail culture what his contemporary Walt Whitman's *Leaves of Grass* was to American poetry—an organic, encyclopedic, periodically expanded redefinition of an art form. And most of its recipes called for ice.

In the nineteenth century, ice came in four main forms: block ice, cubed or lump ice, cracked ice, and shaved ice (also known as "snow"). It's best to think of each of those varieties as being extracted from the previous form. A skilled ice worker or barman would employ an array of tools, from a pick to break up blocks to an ice hammer to crack lumps, and a rasp to collect shavings. Because smaller pieces of ice melt sooner, one had to be careful about measuring out portions as well. In the great bartending manuals, there is no agreed-on discourse of ice. While such terms as *cracked ice* and *snow* were common, in Harry Johnson's 1888 *Bartender's Manual,* for instance, one finds instead "small pieces," which is finely cracked ice, and "fine ice," which is apparently shaved ice in pieces sufficiently bigger than snow to provide a different texture to the drink.

This thoroughness about ice in all its forms was not at all frivolous. Ice is an essential ingredient in so many drinks—strained cocktails, as well as those served on the rocks or frozen. As it melts, ice softens the burn of alcohol and actually blends and opens up the flavors in the drink. The surface area and density of the ice makes a difference as well. As an experiment, try mixing a classic drink—a martini, for example—without ice, just using chilled ingredients, and see how it tastes.

In the twentieth century, as electric freezers and refrigerators became widely available, ice changed. The dominant form of ice became substantial cubes frozen in trays and released with a lever (in the case of metal trays) or a twist (with plastic ones). These old-school cubes are perfect starting points for most drinks. Not only do they melt more slowly than skimpier versions that come from standard hotel ice machines, or the oddly shaped ones from refrigerator ice makers, they also make an undeniably satisfying sound in a glass, and they just look right. In the Coen brothers' homage to classic gangster films, *Miller's Crossing,* exquisite

attention is paid to the tumble and clink of sturdy cubes being loaded into an old-fashioned glass—it's an aesthetically charged, richly ritualistic event.

But let's not stretch that too far. Nowadays, in some of the more esoterically inclined speakeasy bars and glamorous watering holes, ice cubes have been fetishized to the point of absurdity. Specially sourced water, catalogs of shapes and densities—there's no need to go to these lengths, certainly not at home. And if you're making proper frozen cocktails, it's a moot point anyway.

THE RISE OF ICE

And that brings us to the advent of the frozen cocktail. In the nineteenth century, drinks heavily loaded with shaved ice, or snow, were commonplace. One typical mint julep recipe, as preserved by the Southern novelist Walker Percy, involves pouring a healthy dose of sugar in a chilled highball glass, inserting a sprig of mint, and packing the glass completely with shaved ice before filling the arrangement with bourbon. As in so many other aspects of modern life, however, technology opened up new possibilities.

In this case, it was the invention of the electric blender. It took more than 15 years for the countertop (as opposed to immersion) blender to become a household item. The first one, invented in 1922 by Stephen Poplawski, was meant for making milk shakes. Poplawski's concept was picked up by the Hamilton Beach Company, which had been testing how to use a lightweight electric motor to power household appliances since its establishment in 1911 by L. H. Hamilton, Chester Beach, and Fred Osius. Osius made it his mission to develop the electric blender for the household market.

In 1935, having finally managed a workable design for the blender, Osius went in search of investors. He found one in Fred Waring, a famed bandleader with a fondness for gadgets. The story goes that Osius managed to charm his way into Waring's dressing room after a

New York concert and walked out with a commitment of $25,000 for further testing and development. When Osius couldn't manage to produce a reliable enough prototype, Waring took control of the product and had other engineers tinker with the design. In 1938, the Waring Blendor (purposely spelled with an "o" for distinctiveness) entered the market.

The global catastrophe of World War II slowed Waring's business development, but it also made the United States a superpower. Returning servicemen and women, and women who had taken up careers on the home front during the war, looked forward to a postwar America of predictable domestic life, economic growth, and the convenience of new technologies. It was the dawn of a new consumerism, and the public was now deluged with advertisements for trendy new appliances. The Waring Blendor's time had come; by 1954, over a million had been sold.

BLENDED FROZEN COCKTAILS

It didn't take long for blended frozen cocktails to appear. Because rum had remained widely available during the war despite rationing, many of those new drinks were chilly adaptations of Cuban classics: frozen daiquiris and other variations on the theme of rum, fruit, and ice whirled into a slushy, often colorful, concoction. In the 1960s, after revolution removed Cuba from the list of American vacation spots, other "tropical" ingredients began to appear in all sorts of cocktails, but especially ones meant for sultry summer weather. Even the exotic fruits discovered by soldiers in Vietnam played a role.

In the 1970s, cocktails became part of the singles scene, and bartenders devised even more confectionary recipes to appeal to liberated women enjoying more freewheeling social and romantic lives. Frozen blended drinks were part of the picture. (A reference to the venerable Waring Blendor in Warren Zevon's satirical 1976 song "Poor Poor Pitiful Me" testified to that appliance's frequent use.) But there was a downside to this turn in frozen cocktails, and it took two forms. The first was the encounter between frozen cocktails and commercial cocktail mixes, which led to a market saturated with cloying, artificially flavored and colored alternatives to a well-made drink. The second was the gradual association of frozen and overly sweet cocktails with the more tacky excesses of the era. As 1979 gave way to 1980, the number-one single on the U.S. charts was Rupert Holmes's "Escape (The Piña Colada Song)." Never had a mixed drink suffered such a dismal fate.

But starting in the 1980s, and slowly but steadily through the following decade, classic cocktails started to regain cultural currency. The "craft cocktail" movement of recent years, spurred partly by nostalgia and partly by an increasing focus by shrewd marketers on the artisanal and the boutique, has led to a cocktail renaissance. From speakeasy-style watering holes to revitalized hotel bars, enthusiasts are savoring classic cocktails and new variations made from a near-overwhelming array of options on the spirits shelf, increasingly mixed with fresh juices and old-school bitters. Frozen cocktails have shaken off the stigma they picked up in the 1980s, and a new generation of celebrity bartenders are conjuring new recipes as subtle and refined as they are bracing and refreshing. So let's get down to mixing.

TOOLS & TECHNIQUES

To make great frozen cocktails you must first gather the right tools.

BREAKING THE ICE

Along with ice cream, sherbet, and other components of a frozen cocktail, be sure to stock your freezer with proper ice cube trays for iced drinks. For blended frozen drinks, any shape of ice will do, but remember that you should never put whole ice cubes in a blender, no matter how powerful its motor might be. Always use crushed ice, which you can make yourself the old-fashioned way by wrapping chunks or cubes of ice in a bar or kitchen towel and pounding it with the back of a heavy spoon or even the flat of a hammer.

THE BLENDER

There are plenty of good manufacturers out there, so choose a blender that appeals to your sense of design, gets good online reviews, is easy to clean, and functions at a range of speeds. It's important to keep in mind some basic blender techniques as well. First, layer your ingredients in the right order: add liquid (usually chilled) first, followed by the fruit or other solids.

This leads to our second point: keep in mind that, whatever the drink, the ice should be added last—that way the more flavorful ingredients are quickly and smoothly blended together, and the ice doesn't melt too much. Third, never go from zero to sixty, so to speak. Start at a low speed and gradually work your way up to a moderately high spin—you should rarely blend a frozen drink at top speed. And finally, unless you want to wipe sticky drink residue from yourself and surfaces all around you, remember to keep the lid on until the blender blades come to a complete stop.

SHAKERS AND OTHER BAR TOOLS

A well-equipped bar or kitchen also includes less technologically advanced tools. A durable jigger with clearly marked measurements—in ounces, preferably—is a must, as are a cutting board, paring knife, and juicer. Always have at least one long cocktail spoon on hand for stirring iced drinks in tall glasses. A muddler—which is a long wooden pestle—is ideal for extracting flavor from ingredients mingled in the bottom of a glass. If you don't have a muddler, usually a wooden spoon will serve well enough.

For drinks that call for a cocktail shaker, you can choose the two-piece Boston shaker that consists of a metal bottom and glass or plastic mixing glass. For this kind of shaker you will also need a separate sieve for pouring cocktails that call for straining. The other most popular option is the cobbler shaker, a three-piece shaker with a built-in strainer. Even though you won't be straining many drinks presented in this book, you should stock both a coil strainer and a julep strainer. And when you do shake rather than blend or build a drink, make sure that you shake it like you mean it—not violently, but certainly for at least 20 seconds.

THE INGREDIENTS

Although ice can bring out the best in other ingredients, it adds (hopefully) no flavor of its own. Flavor begins with spirits. As with any kind of cocktail, use the best spirits for the frozen drink in question without going overboard. For instance, rums, especially dark and gold rums, should be of excellent quality; that said, don't buy a premier sipping rum and mix it into a piña colada where its flavor will get lost. That's just a waste of a superb spirit.

The same principle goes for other basic flavorings—choose the best available. Use fresh juices whenever possible, for example. They make a breathtaking difference in any drink. The same isn't necessarily true for berries, though. Frozen berries of all kinds can make a lovely blended frozen drink, and they even allow you to use a bit less ice.

As for other sweet flavors, make your own simple sugar. It's easy: equal parts white sugar and plain hot water. Just put them together in a clean lidded jar, shake it well, let it cool, and keep it in your refrigerator, where it will last several days. If you like, you can experiment with alternative sweet syrups, such as agave nectar, which blends well and tastes good, but doesn't have a high glycemic index.

GLASSWARE BASICS

Presentation is important with cocktails, and never more so than with frozen ones. The recipes in this book suggest particular glasses to go with particular drinks. It would be best to follow them if you can, but don't feel as though you've failed at mixology because you don't have a hurricane glass on hand—any tall glass will do in a pinch. Your task will actually be much easier in certain ways than that of pre-Prohibition bartenders, who had to keep track of literally dozens of shapes and styles of glassware.

On the other hand, back in those glory days of cocktails, a barman wouldn't have had to worry about margarita glasses that might hold anywhere from 6 to 20 ounces. Mixing drinks nowadays means working with glasses that, no matter what their shapes, come in all sorts of sizes. Usually, the best policy is to err on the minimalist side: smaller glasses are more gemlike and elegant, they suit the amounts and proportions of the classic recipes, and they don't hold so much alcohol that friends can't buy each other a round without worrying about the effects. That said, the shapes best suited to frozen cocktails—especially hurricane glasses and parfait glasses—already add a festive sense of scale. Still, as with every other aspect of mixology, feel free to experiment. You can devise your own variations on frozen cocktails and craft distinctive presentations for them.

Represented here are some of the glass shapes most frequently recommended for frozen cocktails, along with the range of ounces each type generally holds.

| BOLO GRANDE | BRANDY SNIFTER | CHAMPAGNE COUPE |
| 12–17 OZ | 6–8 OZ | 6–8 OZ |

| CHAMPAGNE FLUTE | CHAMPAGNE TULIP | COCKTAIL GLASS |
| 7–11 OZ | 7–11 OZ | 3–6 OZ |

COLLINS GLASS
10–15 OZ

ICED TEA GLASS
16 OZ

GOBLET
11–16 OZ

HIGHBALL GLASS
8–12.5 OZ

HURRICANE GLASS
10–15.5 OZ

MARGARITA GLASS
6–20 OZ

MARTINI GLASS
4.5–12 OZ

OLD FASHIONED/ROCKS GLASS
6–8 OZ

PARFAIT GLASS
10–20 OZ

PILSNER GLASS
10–14 OZ

SOUR GLASS
3–6 OZ

WINE GLASS
8.5–17 OZ

FINISHING TOUCHES

Garnishes add the finishing touch to a cocktail. Essential to good presentation, their style also sets a mood and displays a bit of personality, whether understated and elegant, or loud and flamboyant.

Garnishes should be fresh and appealing, so use them generously. Some, such as pineapple wedges or mint, can add considerable flavor. Others, such as the salt on the rim of a frozen margarita, bring out the flavors of the other ingredients.

And don't forget the extras: flower petals, paper umbrellas, and festive swizzle sticks all add character to your cocktails.

FROZEN COCKTAIL MAINSTAYS

Many of the recipes in this book will incorporate at least one of four standard fruit garnishes: maraschino cherries, limes, lemons, and oranges. Many will also call for a topping of whipped cream. It never hurts to keep these mainstays on hand.

Maraschino Cherries

Maraschino cherries, often called cocktail cherries, add a pop of color and sweetness, and give a cocktail feel to nonalcoholic drinks. These preserved, sweetened cherries work especially well with cocktails that include grenadine— and they are a traditional topper to whipped cream.

Lemons, Limes, and Oranges

Both lemon and lime add tart freshness to a drink, while orange adds a hint of bright sweetness. These citrus stars are the garnishes of choice for many cocktail classics. Recipes usually call for them in three forms: wedges, wheels, and twists.

To create a wedge, simply cut off the ends of the fruit, slice it in half, and then quarter each half. To create a wheel, cut off the ends, and then carefully cut it into slices however thick or thin you desire. Make one cut from an edge to the center so that you can perch the wheel on the edge of a glass.

To create a basic twist, use a vegetable peeler to remove a wide strip of zest. Be sure to remove as little of the pith as possible. To best use a twist and add a bit of aromatic oil to a cocktail, rub it along the rim of the glass, and then give it a quick twist before floating it in the drink.

For a spiral, puncture the skin with a channeling knife (a bar knife with a V-shaped blade), and then drag the knife around the fruit. You can use this as one graceful spiral or cut it into smaller twists.

Whipped Cream

Whipped cream tops off many dessert and tropical-style frozen cocktails. You can easily make fresh whipped cream by beating a cup of heavy cream with two tablespoons of sugar until it forms stiff peaks. You can also purchase it ready-made in tubs or aerosol cans.

GARNISHES GALORE

Many other fruits make tasty and attractive garnishes, including fresh pineapple, which is perfect in tropical-themed cocktails like the Piña Colada.

Strawberries feature as both an ingredient and a garnish in many frozen cocktail recipes. They add color and are a fruity counterpoint to creamy drinks. Sliced bananas enhance many frozen libations, too, especially those that feature banana liqueurs. Just about any fruit will work as a garnish, from the humble apple to the exotic dragonfruit. For eye-catching cocktails, combine two or three fruit varieties in whimsical arrangements.

For sweet dessert cocktails, candy and cookies are a natural choice. Chocolate can be grated or shaved to add on top, or you can sprinkle on cocoa powder. For creamy drinks, a dusting of cinnamon or nutmeg will add warmth. Coffee or espresso beans floated on top of cocktails based on Kahlúa or other coffee-flavored liqueurs make a simple and elegant presentation.

RIMMING A GLASS

Taking a cue from the classic margarita, many drinks are now served in glasses rimmed with coarse salt, as well as other ingredients, such as sugar or cocoa powder, that complement the cocktail of choice. To rim a glass, moisten the edge with a lime or lemon wedge, and then dip it in the coating.

USE YOUR CREATIVITY

Don't be afraid to experiment with garnishes of other ingredients. Instead of mint, for instance, consider using its relative sweet basil. Thyme goes brilliantly with orange flavors. The more you explore, the more variations you'll find. If you want to be a bit more daring,

consider adding a little heat to your frozen drinks. A touch of chili pepper often intensifies the other flavors in the drink by waking up your palate. Similarly, a pinch of salt can extract a fuller, rounder flavor from fruit juices.

Of course you can always vary the base liquor and see what happens. Thanks to the craft cocktail movement, all sorts of intriguing new flavors of spirits and bitters, some old-fashioned and others innovative, have emerged.

Frozen cocktails offer mixologists blank canvases to express themselves, so feel free to tinker with the old standards or let your imagination fly to create your own unique take on finishing touches.

USING THIS BOOK

You're now ready to explore the compendium of recipes that makes up the rest of this book. From poolside confections to sophisticated and even austere frozen libations, you'll find a fascinating range of drinks to explore. So organize your equipment, collect your ingredients, and start engaging in your own alchemy of spirits, juices, and ice. Tinker with existing recipes. Dream up your own recipes. Enjoy the results with friends and loved ones. The possibilities are endless.

PINEAPPLE DAIQUIRI SLUSH (page 36)

RUM-BASED

COCKTAILS

Rum is used as the key ingredient of some of the most
popular frozen drinks, including daiquiris and coladas.
It has a variety of flavors, based on its three basic forms.
White rum (also known as light or silver rum), which is
aged very little if at all, is the most common in mixed and
frozen drinks. Its relatively neutral flavor combines well with
juices, bitters, and other ingredients. Gold rum sees some
in-barrel aging, which adds a deeper color and flavor. Dark
rum is significantly aged in barrels and develops rich flavors
of molasses, vanilla, and even pipe tobacco. Dark rum can
add depth and complexity to a mixed drink, but premium
aged rums are for sipping, not mixing. Overproof rums can
be as much as 80 percent alcohol, and spiced rums add a
distinct sweetness to cocktails. Although some bartenders
maintain that the more fruit-driven the drink, the lighter the
rum, richly flavored rums often work well in punch-style drinks.

CLASSIC PIÑA COLADA

Combine all ingredients in a blender. Blend briefly at high speed. Pour into a chilled hurricane glass or a hollowed-out coconut shell. An extreme garnish is encouraged—the traditional garnish is a pineapple wedge and a maraschino cherry.

3 oz light rum

3 tbsp cream of coconut

3 tbsp crushed pineapples

4 oz crushed ice

LEFT: The national drink of Puerto Rico, the Piña Colada is a cooling concoction that is perfect for a hot climate.

OPPOSITE: A wedge of pineapple and a red cherry—the classic colada garnishes

BELOW: Rum, cream of coconut, and pineapple juice form the base of the many variations of the Piña Colada cocktail.

FLORIDA PIÑA COLADA

Combine all ingredients in a blender, and blend until smooth and creamy. Pour mixture into a hurricane glass. Garnish simply with fresh pineapple.

¾ oz coconut rum

¾ oz dark rum

3 oz pineapple juice

2 splashes orange juice

2 scoops vanilla
  ice cream

¾ oz cream

4 oz crushed ice

Garnish:

fresh pineapple

BRAZILIAN COLADA

Combine all ingredients in a blender or shaker, and blend until smooth. Pour into a hollowed-out coconut shell or a hurricane glass, and garnish with pineapple and mint.

1½ oz premium cachaça

¾ oz white rum

2 oz pineapple juice

¾ oz cream of coconut

¾ oz cream

4 oz crushed ice

Garnish:

fresh pineapple

sprig of mint

BANANA COLADA

Combine all ingredients in a blender, and blend until the drink begins to thicken. Serve in a hurricane glass or a goblet, and garnish extravagantly.

2 oz light rum
½ banana
1 scoop vanilla ice cream
1½ oz pineapple juice
1½ oz cream of coconut
4 oz crushed ice

ABOVE: The addition of banana to the traditional Piña Colada recipe lends this drink a silkier texture than the original.

OPPOSITE: Garnishes add character and a touch of style to cocktails. Colada cocktails are well-known for their tropical-themed garnishes.

LEFT: The tastiest cocktails start with the freshest fruit.

STRAWBERRY-BANANA COLADA

Place the strawberries and bananas in a blender, reserving some for the garnish. Puree them with the crushed ice, and when the mixture is smooth, add the rest of the ingredients. Blend until smooth. Pour into a large glass, and garnish with the reserved strawberries and bananas.

1¼ oz dark rum

2 oz cream of coconut

2 oz strawberries

1 medium banana

8 oz crushed ice

LEFT AND OPPOSITE: With its creamy pink color, the Strawberry-Banana Colada is as pretty as it is flavorful.

BELOW: Soft fruits like bananas and strawberries will puree easily, but to quicken the process, chop any fruit into fairly small pieces before you place them into the blender.

STRAWBERRY COLADA

Combine all ingredients in a blender, and blend until smooth. Pour into a hurricane glass, and garnish with a fresh strawberry.

1¼ oz white rum

1 oz strawberry liqueur

1 oz strawberry puree

1¼ oz cream of coconut

3 oz pineapple juice

1 tsp whipping cream

8 oz crushed ice

Garnish:

fresh strawberry

PIÑA COLADA ROYALE

Rim a hurricane glass with colored sugar. Combine all ingredients except the ice cubes in a blender, and blend until smooth. Fill the sugar-rimmed glass with the ice cubes, and pour in the mixture. Decorate lavishly with a retro tropical-themed garnish.

3 oz white rum

2 oz coconut rum

3 oz crushed pineapples

1 scoop vanilla ice cream

ice cubes

Garnish:

2 tbsp colored sugar

CLASSIC FROZEN DAIQUIRI

Combine all ingredients in a blender. Blend at low speed for five seconds, and then blend at high speed until firm. Pour into a cocktail glass, and serve with a simple garnish.

1½ oz light rum

1 tbsp triple sec

1½ oz lime juice

1 tsp sugar

4 oz crushed ice

HEMINGWAY DAIQUIRI

Combine all ingredients in a blender, and blend until smooth. Serve in a small cocktail or martini glass.

2 oz white rum

1 oz grapefruit juice

juice of ½ fresh lime

2 splashes maraschino cherry juice

4 oz crushed ice

OPPOSITE: Classic Frozen Daiquiri. This simple cocktail has spawned many variations.

LEFT: Writer Ernest Hemingway came up with his own version. A Hemingway Daiquiri is also known as a Papa Doble or Hemingway Special.

BELOW: The Floridita in Havana, Cuba, is the birthplace of the daiquiri and was a favorite haunt of Hemingway.

ABOVE: The Pineapple Daiquiri Slush is a sweet cocktail bursting with fruit flavor.

PINEAPPLE DAIQUIRI SLUSH

Combine all ingredients in a blender. Blend at a low speed just until slushy. Pour into a cocktail glass, and garnish with a fresh pineapple wedge.

2 oz white rum

½ tsp powdered sugar

¾ oz lime juice

1 tsp pineapple syrup

1 slice pineapple

4–8 oz crushed ice

Garnish:

fresh pineapple

FROZEN PINEAPPLE DAIQUIRI

Combine all ingredients in a blender, and blend until smooth. Pour into a hurricane glass, and garnish with fresh pineapple.

1½ oz light rum

4 pineapple chunks

1 tbsp lime juice

½ tsp sugar

4–8 oz crushed ice

Garnish:

fresh pineapple

CREAMY PINEAPPLE DAIQUIRI

Combine frozen limeade and rum in a blender. Add pineapple and ice cream, and blend well. With the blender running, add some of the crushed ice, and continue adding ice until the mixture is smooth and the blender is nearly full. Pour into martini glasses, and garnish each with a pineapple slice and a cherry. Serves 2 to 4.

6 oz light rum

8 slices canned pineapple

6 oz frozen limeade concentrate

3 tbsp vanilla ice cream

4–8 oz crushed ice

Garnish:

fresh pineapple

maraschino cherries

BANANA DAIQUIRI

Combine all ingredients in a blender. Blend at low speed for five seconds, and then blend at high speed until firm. Pour contents into a martini glass, and garnish simply with a banana slice or lavishly with other fruit.

1½ oz light rum

1 tbsp triple sec

1 medium banana

1½ oz lime juice

1 tsp sugar

4 oz crushed ice

LEFT: For the smoothest and richest-tasting drink, use fresh, fully ripened bananas, which will break down easily even if you use a handheld immersion blender.

BELOW AND OPPOSITE: A Banana Daiquiri can be presented with extravagant garnishes, including the tropical paper umbrellas or pinwheels, or more subdued, with just a fresh slice of banana.

AVOCADO DAIQUIRI

Remove the stone, and peel the avocado.
Combine all ingredients in a blender,
and blend until smooth. Serve in a small
champagne coupe, and garnish with a sprig
of fresh mint.

2 oz light rum

¼ medium avocado

½ oz half-and-half

1 oz fresh lime juice

4 oz crushed ice

Garnish:

sprig of mint

DERBY DAIQUIRI

Combine all ingredients in a blender, and blend at low speed until smooth. Pour into a cocktail glass, and garnish with a lime wheel.

1½ oz light rum

1 oz orange juice

1 tbsp lime juice

1 tsp sugar

4 oz crushed ice

Garnish:

lime wheel

FROZEN BLUE DAIQUIRI

Combine all ingredients in a blender. Blend at low speed for five seconds, and then blend at high speed until firm. Pour contents into a margarita glass, and garnish with orange and lime wheels.

2 oz white rum

½ oz blue curaçao

½ oz lime juice

4 oz crushed ice

Garnish:

lime wheel

orange wheel

FROZEN PEACH DAIQUIRI

Peel and halve the peach, and remove the stone. Combine all ingredients in a blender, and blend until slushy. Serve in a margarita glass, and garnish simply.

1½ oz light rum

¾ oz orange curaçao

½ oz peach schnapps

¾ oz lime juice

½ tsp sugar

½ fresh peach

4 oz crushed ice

LEFT: Pairing fresh peaches with peach schnapps imparts a rich fruit flavor.

BELOW: The elegant Frozen Peach Daiquiri is great for sipping on summer afternoons when the fruit is in season.

BLUEBERRY DAIQUIRI

Blend the blueberries to a puree, and then rub through a sieve to extract the pips. Place the puree back into the blender, add the rest of the ingredients, and blend until smooth. Pour into a hurricane glass, and serve with a fanciful garnish.

1 oz rum

2 oz blueberries

1 oz simple syrup

¼ tbsp lemon juice

½ tbsp lime juice

4 oz crushed ice

RASPBERRY DAIQUIRI

Reserving two to use as a garnish, blend the raspberries to a puree, and then rub through a sieve to extract the pips. Place the puree back into the blender, add the rest of the ingredients, and blend until smooth. Pour into a chilled hurricane glass, and garnish with the reserved raspberries, fresh blueberries, and a lime wheel.

1½ oz light rum

8 oz fresh raspberries

¾ oz lime juice

1 tbsp lemon juice

½ tsp sugar

4 oz crushed ice

Garnish:

fresh blueberries

lime wheel

45

STRAWBERRY DAIQUIRI

Combine four of the strawberries with the rest of the ingredients, and blend until smooth. Strain into a chilled cocktail glass, and garnish with the remaining strawberry.

1½ oz light rum

5 strawberries

1½ oz lemon juice

1 oz lime juice

1 tsp sugar

4 oz crushed ice

LEFT: You can double or triple the ingredients to make a batch of Strawberry Daiquiris. You can also serve it island style, in a larger glass, such as a hurricane or iced tea glass. Add about a half ounce of strawberry liqueur or schnapps to kick up the flavor.

OPPOSITE AND BELOW: A classic frozen Strawberry Daiquiri, one of the most sensuous of all frozen cocktails. You can dress it up with flamboyant garnishes, or serve it with a single strawberry.

FROZEN MINT DAIQUIRI

Combine all ingredients in a blender, and blend until smooth and slushy. Serve in a highball glass decorated with a lime wheel and a sprig of mint.

2 oz light rum

1 tbsp lime juice

6 mint leaves

1 tsp sugar

6 oz crushed ice

Garnish:

lime wheel

sprig of mint

MINT FREEZE DAIQUIRI

Rim a chilled cocktail glass with sugar. Combine all ingredients except the ice cubes in a blender, and blend briefly. Strain the mixture into the sugar-rimmed glass, add the ice cubes, and then garnish lavishly.

2 oz white rum

¼ oz orange liqueur

½ tsp powdered sugar

½ oz lime juice

5 mint leaves

4 oz crushed ice

ice cubes

Garnish:

2 tbsp sugar

FRUIT SALAD DAIQUIRI

Combine all ingredients in a blender, and blend at low speed. Pour into a margarita glass, and serve with a festive garnish.

2 oz light rum

1 oz dark rum

1 tbsp simple syrup

½ tsp powdered sugar

½ small banana

5 chunks pineapple

4 strawberries

¾ oz lime juice

4 oz crushed ice

LEFT AND OPPOSITE: The Fruit Salad Daiquiri blends three tropical drink staples: bananas, strawberries, and pineapples.

BELOW: Don't feel limited to the staple fruits. Just about any fruit makes a delicious daiquiri, so take advantage of what is in season.

BLUE HAWAIIAN

Combine all ingredients in a blender, and blend at high speed until smooth. Pour contents into a hurricane glass. Decorate with a slice of pineapple and a cherry.

1 oz light rum

2 oz pineapple juice

1 oz blue curaçao

1 oz cream of coconut

4 oz crushed ice

Garnish:

fresh pineapple

maraschino cherry

BLUE LAGOON

Combine all ingredients in a blender, and
blend until smooth. Pour mixture into
a hurricane glass, and decorate with a
tropical-themed garnish.

¾ oz white rum

¾ oz dark rum

½ oz blue curaçao

3 oz orange juice

3 oz pineapple juice

1 dash Angostura bitters

4 oz crushed ice

MIAMI WHAMMY

Combine all ingredients in a blender, and blend until smooth. Pour into a hurricane glass, and adorn with a grandiose garnishment of fresh fruit.

2 oz light rum

½ oz orange liqueur

1 oz orange juice

1 oz lemon juice

1 oz grenadine

1 splash papaya juice

4 oz crushed ice

KOKOMO JOE

Combine all ingredients in a blender, and blend until smooth. Pour contents into a parfait or margarita glass, and garnish with wedges of orange and lime.

1 oz light rum

1 oz banana liqueur

5 oz orange juice

2 oz pineapple juice

½ banana

8 oz crushed ice

Garnish:
lime wedges
orange wedge

MEDITERRANEAN ICE

Combine all ingredients in a blender, and blend until thick and slushy. Pour mixture into an old-fashioned glass, and garnish with a star anise.

1½ oz light rum

¼ oz Pernod

4 oz crushed ice

Garnish:

star anise

TANZANIAN TONIC

Combine all ingredients in a blender, and blend until smooth. Pour into iced tea glasses or goblets, and add an extra splash of dark rum to each. Serves 2.

6 oz light rum

1 oz dark rum

4 oz pineapple juice

4 oz apricot nectar

4 oz peach nectar

2 oz lemon juice

2 oz orange juice

1 oz grenadine

4 oz crushed ice

JAMAICAN BANANA

Combine all ingredients in a blender, and blend briefly. Pour contents into a pilsner glass, and top with the sliced banana.

½ oz light rum

½ oz crème de cacao

½ oz crème de bananes

2 scoops vanilla
  ice cream

Garnish:

sliced banana

ICEBREAKER

Combine all ingredients in a blender, and blend until smooth and slushy. Pour into small cocktail glasses, and garnish each with a lemon wedge. Serves 2.

1 oz light rum

1 oz fruit punch

½ oz banana liqueur

¾ oz peach schnapps

4 oz crushed ice

Garnish:

lemon wedge

FROZEN MAI TAI

Combine all ingredients except the
151-proof rum and the ice cubes in a
cocktail shaker. Strain over the ice cubes
into a hurricane or iced tea glass. Float the
151-proof rum on top, and then garnish
extravagantly. For a slushy texture, pour over
additional crushed ice rather than cubes.

1 oz light rum

1 oz dark rum

1 oz fresh lime juice

½ oz orange curaçao

¼ oz orgeat syrup

¼ oz simple syrup

**1 oz 151-proof rum
(optional)**

4 oz crushed ice

ice cubes

LEFT: The Mai Tai can be
found at resorts and tiki bars
throughout the world.

BELOW AND OPPOSITE: Although
associated with Polynesian
settings, the Mai Tai is a
California creation, probably
making its first appearance in
1944 at Trader Vic's. There are
now scores of variations of the
original recipe.

COCOBANANA

Chop the banana, reserving a slice to use with the garnish, and combine it with the rest of the ingredients in a blender. Blend until smooth and creamy. Pour into martini glasses, and garnish with fresh kiwi and the reserved banana. Serves 2.

1 oz white rum

1 oz crème de bananes

½ oz coconut rum

½ oz amaretto

3 oz pineapple juice

1 oz cream of coconut

½ small banana

3 tbsp vanilla
    ice cream

4 oz crushed ice

Garnish:

fresh kiwi

KEY WEST SONG

Combine all ingredients in a blender, and blend until frothy. Pour contents into a martini glass, and garnish with a maraschino cherry and a sprig of mint.

1¼ oz Captain Morgan Silver spiced rum

1 oz cream of coconut

2 oz orange juice

4 oz crushed ice

Garnish:

sprig of mint

maraschino cherry

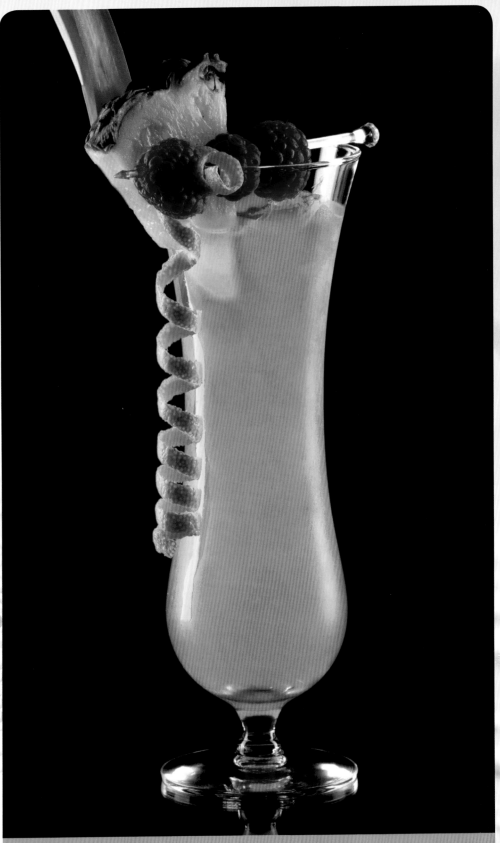

Rum Runner Island Style. According to legend, a bartender at the Holiday Isle Tiki Bar in Islamorada, Florida, first came up with the Rum Runner in the late 1950s. Since then, it has become a standard cocktail, and many variations—including frozen versions—have entered the mixologist's repertoire. Whatever the recipe, this drink calls for a fanciful and eye-catching garnish.

ORIGINAL RUM RUNNER

Combine all ingredients in a blender, and blend thoroughly. Pour the mixture into a tall glass, and decorate with an ornate garnish.

1 oz 151-proof rum

1 oz blackberry brandy

1 oz banana liqueur

1½ oz fresh lime juice

1 splash grenadine

6 oz crushed ice

FLORIDA RUM RUNNER

Combine all ingredients except the 151-proof rum in a blender, and blend thoroughly. Pour the mixture into a tall glass, and then float the 151-proof rum on top. Garnish extravagantly.

1 oz light rum

1 oz dark rum

1 oz blackberry liqueur

1 oz banana liqueur

1 oz pineapple juice

1 oz orange juice

1 dash pomegranate syrup

1 oz 151-proof rum (optional)

6 oz crushed ice

RUM RUNNER ISLAND STYLE

Combine all ingredients except the ice cubes in a blender, and blend thoroughly. Pour into a tall glass over the ice cubes, and decorate elaborately with a mix of fruit or other tropical-themed garnishes.

1 oz dark rum

1 oz light rum

½ oz blackberry liqueur

¼ oz banana liqueur

1 splash grenadine

1 splash lime juice

6 oz crushed ice

ice cubes

TAHITI FLIP

Pour all ingredients except the crushed ice into a cocktail shaker, and shake well. Add the ice, and shake again until frothy and thoroughly chilled. Strain the mixture into a chilled margarita glass, and garnish with a fresh strawberry.

1½ oz white rum

½ oz triple sec

¼ oz limoncello liqueur

¼ oz Campari

½ oz fresh lemon juice

1 large egg white

2 oz crushed ice

Garnish:

fresh strawberry

SHARK ATTACK

Combine all ingredients except the grenadine in a blender. Blend until slushy. Pour into a highball glass, and add the grenadine. Serve with a straw, but do not stir.

1½ oz dark rum

3 oz orange juice

½ oz sour mix

¾ oz grenadine

4 oz crushed ice

PARROT PERCH

Combine all ingredients in a blender, and blend until smooth. Pour contents into a hurricane glass. Top with whipped cream, and serve with a lavish garnish.

1½ oz coconut rum

½ oz triple sec

1 banana

3 oz orange juice

1 oz banana syrup

4 oz crushed ice

Garnish:

whipped cream

PAPAYA PARADISE

Cut the papaya into small pieces, and puree in a blender. Add the rest of the ingredients, and blend until smooth. Pour into a parfait glass, and garnish with an orange wheel and a maraschino cherry. Serves 4.

8 oz dark rum

1 ripe papaya

6 oz half-and-half

2 tbsp sugar

3 strawberries

4 oz crushed ice

Garnish:

orange wheel

maraschino cherry

FROZEN FLAME

Combine all ingredients in a blender, and blend until slushy. Pour contents into a tall glass, and serve unadorned.

1 oz rum

1 oz apricot brandy

½ oz dark rum

½ oz triple sec

3 oz fresh orange juice

1 splash grenadine

4 oz crushed ice

LAVA FLOW

Reserve a strawberry for the garnish, and then place the rums and the strawberries in a hurricane glass. Muddle them together until they form a smooth paste. Combine the rest of the ingredients in a blender, and blend until smooth. Slowly pour into the glass so that the strawberry mixture oozes its way along the sides of the glass, creating the flowing lava effect. Top with whipped cream, a lime twist, and the reserved strawberry.

1 oz light rum

1 oz coconut rum

2 oz strawberries

1 banana

2 oz pineapple juice

2 oz cream of coconut

4 oz crushed ice

Garnish:

whipped cream

lime twist

BATIDA DE PIÑA

Combine all ingredients in a blender, and blend until smooth. Pour contents into a large highball or hurricane glass, and garnish with a spear of fresh pineapple.

2½ oz cachaça
¾ cup crushed pineapple
½ tsp superfine sugar
4 oz crushed ice

Garnish:
fresh pineapple

BATIDA DE MARACUJA

Combine all ingredients in a blender, reserving one of the chunks of passion fruit. Blend until smooth. Pour contents into a large glass, and garnish with the reserved passion fruit and a sprig of mint.

¾ oz cachaça
2 oz pineapple juice
¼ oz lime syrup
1 tsp lime juice
2 passion fruit chunks
4 oz crushed ice

Garnish:
sprig of mint

BATIDA FROZEN

Combine all ingredients in a blender, and blend until smooth. Strain contents into a highball glass, and garnish with a lime wheel.

2 oz cachaça
2 oz frozen tropical-fruit puree
1 oz sweetened condensed milk
1 oz simple syrup
4 oz crushed ice

Garnish:
lime wheel

BATIDA DE CARNEVAL

Combine all ingredients in a blender, and blend until smooth. Pour contents into a large highball glass, and garnish with a slice of fresh mango.

¾ oz cachaça
1 oz orange juice
2¼ oz mango juice
4 oz crushed ice

Garnish:
fresh mango

A Batida de Piña. A batida, which means "shaken" or "milk shake" in Portuguese, is a cocktail made with cachaça. Often referred to as Brazilian rum, cachaça is made exclusively in Brazil. It can be a harsh liquor, but premium brands, such as Sagatiba Pura and Leblon, are smooth and sweet.

APPLE PIE

Combine all ingredients in a blender, and blend until frothy. Pour contents into a champagne flute, float the chopped apples on top, and garnish with a sprinkle of ground cinnamon.

1 oz dark rum

2 oz apple juice

½ oz cream of coconut

4 oz crushed ice

Garnish:

2 tbsp chopped apple

ground cinnamon

APPLE PIE À LA MODE

Combine all ingredients except the ice cream in a blender, and blend until smooth. Pour contents into an old-fashioned glass. Float the ice cream on top, and garnish with a star anise and a cinnamon stick.

1 oz dark rum

2 oz apple juice

½ oz cream of coconut

½ scoop vanilla ice cream

4 oz crushed ice

Garnish:

star anise

cinnamon stick

PINK ESKIMO

Peel the pineapple, and chop it into chunks. Peel and slice the apple, making sure to discard the seeds, and peel the orange, again making sure to discard seeds. In a blender, combine the fruit with all the remaining ingredients. Pour into hurricane glasses or goblets and serve with a cherry garnish. Serves 2.

½ oz light rum

8 oz coconut rum

½ pineapple

1 green apple

1 orange

18 oz raspberry yogurt

3 oz orange juice

2 tbsp lemon juice

6 oz crushed ice

Garnish:

maraschino cherries

COO COO

Combine all ingredients in a blender, and blend until smooth. Pour into a hurricane glass or a goblet, and garnish with a fresh orange wheel.

1½ oz rum

1½ oz Midori
melon liqueur

3 oz Piña Colada mix

3 oz sweet and sour mix

4 oz crushed ice

Garnish:
orange wheel

PICKER'S PEACH

Reserving a slice of peach for the garnish, combine all ingredients in a blender, and blend until smooth. Pour into a margarita glass, and garnish with the reserved peach.

1½ oz light rum

½ oz dark rum

1 oz peach schnapps

1 tsp peach liqueur

1 oz orange juice

¾ oz lemon juice

½ tsp superfine sugar

½ small ripe peach

4 oz crushed ice

CAPE CODDER

Combine all ingredients except the ice cubes in a blender, and blend briefly. Pour contents into a chilled glass filled with the ice cubes. Garnish with a lime wedge.

1½ oz light rum

3 oz cranberry juice

½ oz fresh lime juice

4 oz crushed ice

ice cubes

Garnish:

lime wedge

MERRY GENTLEMAN

Combine all ingredients in a blender, and blend until smooth and slushy. Pour contents into a hurricane glass, and decorate with a black raspberry and a lime wedge.

3 oz light rum

2 oz strawberries

2 oz blueberries

1 oz lime juice

1 tsp simple syrup

4 oz crushed ice

Garnish:

fresh black raspberry

lime wedge

METEOR MAKER

Peel and stone the mango, and then combine all ingredients in a blender. Blend until smooth. Pour contents into a highball glass, and serve with a simple garnish.

2 oz dark rum

1 oz white rum

½ oz simple syrup

1 mango

½ oz lime juice

81

LETHAL LEMONADE

Rim a chilled martini glass with colored sugar. Pour ingredients into a cocktail shaker, and shake until thoroughly chilled. Pour into the sugar-rimmed glass, and garnish with the lime wheel.

6 oz light rum

6 oz frozen lemonade concentrate

8 oz crushed ice

Garnish:

2 tbsp colored sugar

lime wheel

CRIME OF PASSION

Combine all ingredients except the cream soda in a blender. Blend until frothy. Pour into a martini glass, and add soda. Garnish with an orange twist and fresh raspberries.

1 oz dark rum

1 oz passion fruit juice

2 tbsp vanilla ice cream

½ oz raspberry syrup

3 oz cream soda

Garnish:

orange twist

fresh raspberries

MANGO MINT

Combine all ingredients in a blender with crushed ice, and blend at low speed for about 15 seconds. Pour contents into a margarita glass, and garnish with mint.

1 oz light rum

1½ oz mango nectar

2 tsp white crème de menthe

4 oz crushed ice

Garnish:

mint leaves

MANGO MADNESS

Peel and stone the mango, and then combine with the rum and mango syrup in a blender. Blend until smooth. Strain into an iced tea glass filled with crushed ice, and then stir until the ice is blended. Squeeze in the lime juice, and serve.

¾ oz white rum

¾ oz mango syrup

¼ mango

juice of ¼ fresh lime

4 oz crushed ice

FROSTY ZOMBIE

Combine all ingredients except the 151-proof rum in a blender. Blend until the mixture is about half ice slush and half liquid on the bottom. Pour into a large highball or hurricane glass, and lace with the 151-proof rum. Garnish extravagantly.

1½ oz golden rum

½ oz light rum

1 oz dark rum

½ oz 151-proof rum

1 oz fresh lime juice

½ oz pineapple juice

1 splash papaya juice

1 splash grenadine

4 oz crushed ice

FROZEN KEY LIME PIE

Combine all ingredients in a blender, and
blend until smooth. Serve in a martini glass,
and garnish with a lime twist.

1 oz white rum

½ oz dark rum

½ oz orange liqueur

1½ oz lime juice

3 tbsp vanilla

4 oz crushed ice

Garnish:

lime twist

MOOSE MILK

Combine all ingredients in a blender until the mixture appears to have the consistency of a milk shake. Pour into large drinking glasses, and garnish each with whole cinnamon sticks or sprinkle with cinnamon or nutmeg. Serves approximately 2 to 4.

2 oz white rum

2 oz dark rum

2 oz Kahlúa

2 oz amaretto

2 oz Irish cream liqueur

4 scoops vanilla
 ice cream

Garnish:

cinnamon or nutmeg

FROZEN BANANAS FOSTER

Combine all ingredients in a blender, and blend until smooth. Pour contents into a brandy snifter, and top with whipped cream. Sprinkle ground cinnamon or nutmeg on top.

1½ oz spiced rum

½ oz banana liqueur

1 medium banana

2 scoops vanilla ice cream

1 tsp brown sugar

Garnish:

whipped cream

cinnamon or nutmeg

MALIBU MILK SHAKE

Combine all ingredients in a blender, and blend until smooth. Serve in a highball glass with a sprinkle of ground nutmeg, and complete the look with a luxurious garnish.

4 oz Malibu coconut rum

2 tbsp sugar

8 oz milk

4 oz crushed ice

Garnish:

ground nutmeg

MALIBU PINK PANTHER

Combine the frozen pink lemonade and Malibu rum with the crushed ice, and blend for 30 seconds or until smooth. Add in your desired amount of heavy cream, and blend further until smooth. Pour into a chilled cocktail glass, and garnish extravagantly.

4 oz Malibu coconut rum

1½ oz frozen pink lemonade concentrate

heavy cream to taste

3 oz crushed ice

91

FROZEN MUDSLIDE

Combine all ingredients except the chocolate syrup in a blender, and blend until smooth. Drizzle the chocolate syrup down the inside of the glass of your choice, and pour mixture inside. Garnish as simply or as flamboyantly as you desire.

2 oz light rum

2 oz Kahlúa

2 oz Irish cream liqueur

4 scoops vanilla
ice cream

1 oz chocolate syrup

LEFT: Presentation is everything, and the same cocktail served in a different kind of glass will set a different mood. Hurricane and pilsner glasses seem to demand a bit of whimsy, with lots of whipped cream and even a curly straw.

BELOW LEFT: A margarita glass still sets a fun mood.

BELOW AND OPPOSITE: Even a frivolous cocktail like the Frozen Mudslide can have an air of sophistication when served in an elegant martini glass or champagne flute with only subtle garnishes.

SASQUATCH

Combine all ingredients in a blender, and blend until smooth. Serve in a large glass decorated with a light-hearted garnish.

6 oz light rum

6 oz frozen limeade concentrate

8 pineapple chunks

2 scoops vanilla ice cream

4 oz crushed ice

JEDI MIND TRICK

Combine all ingredients in a blender, and blend until smooth. Pour into a chilled hurricane glass, and serve.

1 oz dark rum

1 oz amaretto

1 oz Kahlúa

1 oz Baileys Irish Cream

3 scoops vanilla ice cream

SOUTH POLE SUNSHINE

Combine all ingredients in a blender, and blend until smooth. Pour into a highball glass, and garnish with peeled orange.

6 oz light rum

6 oz orange juice

2 oz orange curaçao

4 oz light cream

4 oz crushed ice

Garnish:

fresh peeled orange

POLAR COOLER

Combine all ingredients in a blender, and blend until smooth. Pour contents into a parfait or hurricane glass, and decorate with a lavish fruit garnish.

1½ oz light rum

1 oz orange liqueur

½ oz triple sec

1 oz orange juice

½ oz light cream

4 oz crushed ice

FROZEN SNICKERS (page 115)

VODKA-BASED

COCKTAILS

Vodka is a relatively recent arrival in the cocktail world, having gained popularity with the discovery of its Russian version during and after World War II. It might be described as the anti-rum: neutral, cold-climate in origin, and never aged. But its neutrality gives it a wide range as a base spirit—hence its use in such classics as the Vodka Martini, Screwdriver, Black Russian, and Bloody Mary, among others. Traditionally distilled from grains (rye and wheat are considered the best), potato, or even molasses, vodka originated in eastern Europe and became the dominant spirit in most Scandinavian and Slavic countries, where it is normally consumed neat for its clean, bracing quality. But it also works brilliantly when flavored with fruits, herbs, and spices, and in cream-based drinks. Such varieties as citrus vodka, pepper vodka, and vanilla vodka have made for intriguing variations on all sorts of frozen cocktails.

BLACK FOREST SHAKE

Rim a chilled martini glass with cocoa powder, reserving some for the garnish. Allow the ice cream to soften for several minutes, and then combine all ingredients in a blender. Blend until smooth, and then pour into the cocoa-rimmed glass. Top with the reserved cocoa powder and one or two maraschino cherries.

½ oz vodka

½ oz cherry brandy

6 oz milk

2 oz frozen cherries

2 scoops chocolate ice cream

2 oz chocolate chips

Garnish:

2 tbsp cocoa powder

maraschino cherries

RUSSIAN MUDSLIDE

Combine all ingredients except the chocolate syrup in a blender, and blend until smooth. Drizzle the chocolate syrup down the insides of two martini glasses. Pour the mixture into the glasses, and garnish with the maraschino cherries and chocolate shavings. Serves 2.

1½ oz vodka

1½ oz Irish cream liqueur

1½ oz coffee liqueur

1½ oz cream

1 scoop vanilla ice cream

2 scoops chocolate
   ice cream

2 tbsp chocolate syrup

4 oz crushed ice

Garnish:

chocolate shavings

maraschino cherries

BABY JANE

Combine all ingredients in a blender, and blend until smooth. Serve in a cocktail glass, and garnish with a maraschino cherry.

½ oz vodka

½ oz gin

½ oz butterscotch liqueur

½ oz Irish cream liqueur

2 scoops vanilla ice cream

4 oz crushed ice

Garnish:

maraschino cherry

HAMMER HORROR

Combine all ingredients in a blender, and
blend until smooth. Serve in a martini glass,
and sprinkle with grated chocolate.

1 oz vodka

1 oz Kahlúa

4 tbsp vanilla ice cream

Garnish:

grated chocolate

MONKEY LA LA

Combine all ingredients except the chocolate syrup in a blender, and blend until smooth and frothy. Pour mixture into a chilled hurricane glass, and then pour in the chocolate syrup, allowing it to sink down the sides. Top with whipped cream and banana.

1 oz vodka

1 oz Kahlúa

1 oz Irish cream liqueur

½ oz banana liqueur

1 oz pineapple juice

2 oz half-and-half

2 oz cream of coconut

1 scoop vanilla ice cream

1 oz chocolate syrup

2 oz crushed ice

Garnish:

whipped cream

sliced banana

KRETCHMA

Combine all ingredients in a blender, and blend until smooth. Pour into a chilled martini glass, and dust with cocoa powder.

1 oz vodka

1 oz white crème de cacao

½ oz lemon juice

½ tsp grenadine

4 oz crushed ice

Garnish:
cocoa powder

105

NUTCRACKER

Rim a chilled martini glass with colored sugar. Combine all ingredients except the ice cream in a blender, and blend until thoroughly smooth. Pour into the rimmed martini glass, and float the ice cream on top. Add a few candy snowflakes or other edible confetti sprinkles for a seasonal decoration.

1 oz vodka

½ oz Baileys Irish Cream

½ oz amaretto

½ oz Frangelico hazelnut liqueur

1 scoop vanilla ice cream

4 oz crushed ice

Garnish:

2 tbsp colored sugar

edible confetti sprinkles

BLUE CHRISTMAS

Combine all ingredients except the coconut
ice cream in a blender, and blend until
smooth. Pour into a martini glass, and float
the ice cream on top.

1 oz vodka

1½ oz blue curaçao

1 tbsp white crème
de cacao

1 tbsp light cream

1 scoop coconut
ice cream

FROZEN WHITE RUSSIAN

Combine all ingredients in a blender, and
blend until smooth and silky. Pour contents
into an old-fashioned glass, and serve
unadorned or with a simple garnish.

2 oz vanilla vodka

1 oz Kahlúa

1 oz light cream

4 oz crushed ice

FROZEN PINK RUSSIAN

Combine all ingredients in a blender, and blend until smooth. Pour into a chilled martini glass, and drop in a cherry.

1 oz vodka

2 oz strawberry cream liqueur

1 oz Kahlúa

1 oz milk

4 oz crushed ice

Garnish:
maraschino cherry

FROZEN BLACK RUSSIAN

Combine all ingredients in a blender, and blend until frothy. Pour into a martini glass, and float a few coffee beans on top.

1 oz vodka

1 oz Kahlúa

3 oz cola

4 oz crushed ice

Garnish:
coffee beans

ABOVE: Frozen Black Russian. Kahlúa is a rum-based Mexican coffee liqueur flavored with vanilla bean. It is often paired with vodka to make "Russian" cocktails.

CHOCOLATE MARTINI

Rim a chilled martini glass with cocoa powder. Combine the ingredients in a blender, and blend until smooth. Pour contents into the cocoa-rimmed glass, and garnish with chocolate shavings.

1½ oz vodka

¼ oz Kahlúa

¾ oz Godiva liqueur

2 oz crushed ice

Garnish:

2 tbsp cocoa powder

chocolate shavings

WHITE CHOCOLATE MARTINI

Layer the chocolate syrup at the bottom of a martini glass. Combine all other ingredients in a blender, and blend until smooth. Pour the mixture into the glass, and serve with an elegant garnish.

1 oz vanilla vodka

2 oz Godiva white chocolate liqueur

1 oz cream

½ oz white crème de cacao

1 tbsp chocolate syrup

2 oz crushed ice

SILVER FIZZ

Combine all ingredients in a blender, and blend until frothy. Pour into a hurricane glass, and garnish with an orange wheel.

2 oz vodka

2 oz half-and-half

1 tbsp powdered sugar

6 oz frozen pink lemonade concentrate

1 egg

4 oz crushed ice

Garnish:

orange wheel

BLACK MAGIC

Combine all ingredients in a blender, and blend until frothy. Pour into a chilled martini glass. Float a few espresso beans on top, and garnish with an orange twist.

1½ oz vodka

¾ oz coffee liqueur

1 oz lemon juice

4 oz crushed ice

Garnish:

orange twist

espresso beans

FLYING GRASSHOPPER

Combine all ingredients in a blender, and blend until smooth. Pour into a martini glass, and garnish with a sprig of mint.

1 oz vodka

1 oz white crème de cacao

2 oz green crème de menthe

4 oz crushed ice

Garnish:

sprig of mint

FROZEN SNICKERS

Rim a chilled martini glass with cocoa powder. Combine all ingredients in a blender, and blend until smooth. Pour contents into the cocoa-rimmed glass, and garnish with chocolate shavings.

2 oz vodka

1 oz hazelnut liqueur

1 oz white crème de cacao

½ oz cream liqueur

3 oz crushed ice

Garnish:

2 tbsp cocoa powder

chocolate shavings

BANANAS FOSTER MARTINI

Slice the frozen banana, and then combine all ingredients in a blender. Blend until smooth. Pour into a hurricane glass, and garnish with the whipped cream and mint.

2 oz vodka

2 oz chocolate liqueur

1 oz banana liqueur

½ medium banana, frozen

1 scoop vanilla ice cream

Garnish:

whipped cream

sprig of mint

KEY LIME PIE MARTINI

Rim a chilled martini glass with a mixture of the graham cracker crumbs and powdered sugar. Combine all ingredients in a blender, and blend until smooth and creamy. Pour mixture into the rimmed glass, and garnish with a lime wheel.

1½ oz vanilla vodka

1½ oz key lime liqueur

½ oz Rose's lime juice

¼ oz fresh-squeezed lime juice

1½ oz half-and-half

Garnish:

2 tbsp graham cracker crumbs

1 tbsp powdered sugar

lime wheel

ABOVE: Adam Sunrise. Add frozen juice concentrates to a cocktail for instant slush and vibrant flavor.

ADAM SUNRISE

Combine all ingredients in a blender, and blend until smooth and frothy. Pour contents into old-fashioned glasses, and garnish each with a sprig of mint and a lemon wheel. Serves 6.

12 oz vodka

6 oz frozen lemonade concentrate

12 oz water

10 tsp sugar

6 oz crushed ice

Garnish:
lemon wheel
sprig of mint

WHITE LIGHTNING

Combine ingredients in a blender, and blend until smooth and frothy. Pour contents into a collins glass, and serve with a straw.

4 oz vodka

6 oz frozen lemonade concentrate

PEACH FUZZ

Pit and slice two medium ripe peaches, reserving some for the garnish. Combine the sliced peaches with the vodka and limeade in a blender. Blend until smooth, and serve in a hurricane glass garnished with the reserved peach slices.

6 oz vodka

6 oz frozen limeade concentrate

2 medium peaches

BERRY FROST

Combine all ingredients in a blender, and blend until smooth. Pour into a cocktail glass, and garnish with fresh berries and other fruit, if you desire.

2 oz vodka

3 oz frozen lemonade concentrate

1½ oz blackberry liqueur

1½ oz raspberry puree

Garnish:

fresh blackberries

CHILLY MANDARIN

Slice the peach, and blend it with the frozen orange juice and raspberries. Add the grenadine, lime juice, and vanilla extract. Blend until smooth. Pour the orange vodka into a hurricane glass, and fill the glass halfway with the mix from the blender. Add the crushed ice, top up with champagne, and decorate with a fanciful garnish.

1½ oz orange vodka

3 oz champagne

3 drops grenadine

3½ oz frozen orange juice concentrate

1 tsp lime juice

½ fresh peach

½ oz frozen raspberries

2 tbsp vanilla extract

4 oz crushed ice

APPLE JUDY

Combine all ingredients in a blender, and blend until frothy. Serve in a martini glass decorated with apple slices.

½ oz vodka

½ oz Grand Marnier

3 oz apple juice

4 oz crushed ice

Garnish:

fresh apple

FROSTY LEMON DROP

Rim a chilled martini glass with sugar. Combine all ingredients in a blender, and blend until frothy. Pour contents into the sugar-rimmed glass, and garnish with a lemon wedge.

1½ oz vodka

½ oz triple sec

1 tsp superfine sugar

¾ oz fresh-squeezed lemon juice

2 oz crushed ice

Garnish:

2 tbsp granulated sugar

lemon wedge

BLOOD ORANGE MARTINI

Combine all ingredients in a blender, and blend until frothy. Pour into a martini glass and garnish with an orange twist.

2 oz orange vodka

1 oz Campari

1 oz orange juice

4 oz crushed ice

Garnish:

orange twist

RASPBERRY SWIRL

Layer one ounce of the raspberry liqueur at the bottom of a chilled martini glass. Combine the vodka, amaretto, and ice cream in a blender, and blend until thick and creamy. Pour the mixture over the liqueur, and with a straw or swizzle stick, gently swirl the remaining liqueur on top. Garnish with a few fresh raspberries.

1 oz vodka

1 oz amaretto

1 scoop vanilla
    ice cream

1½ oz raspberry liqueur

Garnish:

fresh raspberries

ORANGE FREEZE

Combine all ingredients in a blender, and blend until slushy. Pour into a pilsner or collins glass, and place in freezer for 10 minutes before serving.

2 oz vodka

1 oz rum

4 oz orange juice

4 scoops orange sherbet

BLUEBERRY FREEZE

Combine all ingredients in a blender, and blend until smooth. Pour into a hurricane glass, and garnish with a sprig of mint.

1 oz vodka

¼ oz wildberry schnapps

1 oz cream of coconut

2 oz blueberries

1½ oz crushed pineapple

1 scoop vanilla ice cream

8 oz crushed ice

Garnish:

sprig of mint

WATERMELON VODKA SLUSH

Reserve two chunks of watermelon for the garnish, and then in a food processor, puree the remaining watermelon. Pour into ice cube trays, and freeze for four hours. Combine the frozen watermelon with all other ingredients in a blender, and blend until slushy. Pour into old-fashioned glasses, and garnish each with a slice of watermelon. Serves 2.

4 oz vodka

16 oz watermelon flesh, seeds removed

½ oz simple syrup

1 tbsp lemon juice

1 oz melon liqueur

Garnish:

sprig of mint

PINEAPPLE FROST

Combine all ingredients in a blender, and blend until smooth. Pour into a margarita glass, and garnish with a chunk of pineapple and a green cocktail cherry.

1 oz vanilla vodka

2 oz pineapple juice

4 oz crushed ice

Garnish:
fresh pineapple
green cocktail cherry

SIBERIAN SUNRISE

Pour all ingredients except the grenadine into a cocktail shaker, and shake vigorously until thoroughly chilled. Pour into a martini glass, add grenadine, and serve immediately.

1½ oz vodka

4 oz grapefruit juice

½ oz triple sec

1 splash grenadine

4 oz crushed ice

SOVIET COCKTAIL

Pour all ingredients into a cocktail shaker, and shake until thoroughly chilled. Strain into a chilled cocktail glass. Twist lemon peel over drink, and drop it into the glass.

1½ oz vodka

½ oz dry vermouth

½ oz dry sherry

4 oz crushed ice

Garnish:

lemon peel

COSSACK CHARGE

Pour all ingredients into a cocktail shaker, and shake vigorously until thoroughly chilled. Pour into a chilled martini glass, and drop in a maraschino cherry.

1½ oz vodka

½ oz cognac

½ oz cherry brandy

4 oz crushed ice

Garnish:

maraschino cherry

FROZEN COSSACK COCOA

Rim two chilled champagne flutes with cocoa powder. Combine all ingredients in a blender, and blend until smooth. Pour into the flutes, and garnish with a maraschino cherry. Serves 2.

½ oz vodka

1 oz Kahlúa

½ oz cherry brandy

1 scoop cherry-chocolate
  ice cream

Garnish:

2 tbsp cocoa powder

maraschino cherry

Siberian Sunrise. To add grenadine to any sunrise cocktail without mixing it in, tilt the glass and quickly upend the grenadine bottle, pouring the grenadine down the side of the glass. It will fall to the bottom, and then rise slowly through the drink. You can also use a spoon to guide the syrup downward.

HEARTBREAKER'S SPECIAL

Combine all ingredients in a blender, and blend until slushy. Pour into a martini glass. Garnish with a few fresh cranberries.

2 oz vodka

3 oz Passoã liqueur

1 oz fresh lime juice

1 splash of cranberry juice

4 oz crushed ice

Garnish:

fresh cranberries

HILDE'S SPECIAL

Combine all ingredients in a blender, and blend until smooth. Pour into an old-fashioned glass, and garnish with melon balls.

½ oz vodka

¾ oz melon liqueur

3 oz sweet and sour mix

3 oz crushed ice

Garnish:

fresh melon balls

CHI CHI

Combine all ingredients in a blender, and blend until smooth. Pour into a hurricane or tall glass, and serve with a playful tiki-style garnish.

1½ oz vodka

3½ oz pineapple juice

1 oz cream of coconut

1 oz heavy cream

4 oz crushed ice

CHI CHI BLUE HEAVEN

Allow the ice cream to soften for a few minutes, and then combine all the ingredients in a blender. Blend until smooth. Pour into martini glasses, and garnish as simply or as extravagantly as you desire. Serves 2.

2 oz coconut vodka

½ oz blue curaçao

½ oz cream of coconut

4 oz pineapple juice

1 scoop vanilla
ice cream

OPPOSITE: The Chi Chi is a favorite from the 1950s tiki bar craze.

LEFT: Bottles of vodka. A Chi Chi uses the same ingredients as its cousin the Piña Colada, swapping out rum for vodka.

BELOW: Chi Chi Blue Heaven. Add some blue curaçao to the mix to evoke a tropical paradise.

LAWN BOY

Combine all ingredients in a blender, and blend until frothy. Serve in a martini glass garnished with mint leaves.

2½ oz vodka

3 or 4 mint leaves

¾ oz limeade

½ tsp sugar

2 oz crushed ice

Garnish:

mint leaves

HAWAIIAN MORNING

Combine all ingredients in a blender, and
blend until frothy. Pour into a cocktail glass,
and decorate with a Polynesian-style garnish.

1 oz vodka

1 oz peach liqueur

2 oz pineapple juice

4 oz crushed ice

BLUE BAYOU

Combine all ingredients in a blender, and blend until smooth. Serve in a large chilled cocktail glass, and garnish with a wedge of fresh pineapple.

1½ oz vodka

½ oz blue curaçao

4 oz fresh or canned pineapple

2 oz grapefruit juice

4 oz crushed ice

Garnish:

fresh pineapple

FROZEN BLUE TIKI

Combine all ingredients in a blender, and blend until smooth. Pour into a parfait glass, and decorate with a retro tiki-style garnish.

1 oz vodka

1 oz blue curaçao

2 oz pineapple juice

1 oz cream of coconut

4 oz crushed ice

BLUE HAWAIIAN SCREW

Combine all ingredients in a blender with crushed ice, and blend until smooth. Pour into a margarita glass, and garnish with a pineapple spear and a maraschino cherry.

2 oz vodka

4 oz pineapple juice

1½ oz lemon juice

1 oz simple syrup

1 splash blue curaçao

2 oz crushed ice

Garnish:

fresh pineapple

maraschino cherry

ABOVE: Blue Hawaiian Screw. This version of the tropical mainstay replaces rum with vodka, which imparts a distinct taste of spirit without sweetness. Blue curaçao gives these drinks the color of the sea and sky.

139

ICY BLOODY MARY MARTINI

Rim a chilled martini glass with paprika. Combine all ingredients in a blender with crushed ice, and blend until frothy. Pour contents into the paprika-rimmed glass, and garnish with a grape tomato and celery.

1 oz vodka

3 oz tomato juice

½ oz lemon juice

2 dashes Tabasco sauce

1 dash Worcestershire sauce

2 pinches celery salt

1 pinch black pepper

2 oz crushed ice

Garnish:

2 tbsp paprika

stalk of celery

grape tomato

CREAMY SCREWDRIVER

Combine all ingredients in a blender, and briefly blend at a low speed. Pour into martini glasses, and add straws. Serves 2.

2 oz vodka

6 oz orange juice

1 tsp sugar

1 egg yolk

4 oz crushed ice

JERSEY SHORE

Combine all ingredients in a blender, and
blend until slushy. Pour into a highball
glass, garnish with a sprig of mint, and serve
with a straw.

1 oz strawberry vodka

2 oz cranberry juice

2 oz pomegranate juice

1 oz orange juice

6 oz crushed ice

Garnish:

sprig of mint

DETROIT WINTER

Combine all ingredients in a blender, and blend until smooth. Pour into a hurricane glass, and top with whipped cream and a fresh strawberry.

6 oz orange vodka

1 oz triple sec

4 oz passion fruit juice

2 oz evaporated milk

4 oz crushed ice

Garnish:

whipped cream

fresh strawberry

143

SEX ON ICE

Reserving one of the strawberries for the garnish, combine all ingredients in a blender, and blend until smooth. Pour into a cocktail glass. Top with whipped cream, and garnish with the reserved strawberry.

½ oz vodka
½ oz light rum
½ oz cherry liqueur
½ oz melon liqueur
¼ oz strawberry schnapps
8 oz frozen strawberries

Garnish:
whipped cream

SEX IN THE SNOW

Combine all ingredients in a blender, and blend until slushy. Pour into a cocktail glass, and serve with straws.

3 oz vanilla vodka
¾ oz milk
1 splash cranberry juice
3 oz crushed ice

SNOW BLINDER

Blend vodka and ice cream until smooth. Pour into a margarita glass, and top up with the lemonade. Stir briefly, and garnish with a cherry. Serves 2.

2 oz vodka
2 scoops vanilla
  ice cream
8 oz lemonade

Garnish:
maraschino cherry

ICY POLE

Combine all ingredients in a blender, and blend until slushy. Serve in a goblet or highball glass, and garnish extravagantly.

1 oz vodka
3 oz passion fruit juice
3 oz orange juice
4 oz crushed ice

Sex in the Snow. Cocktails may have always provided a stimulating drinking experience, but in the 1980s, the trend of naming them with titillating titles swept lounges and bars everywhere.

FROZEN JADE

Combine all ingredients in a blender, and blend until slushy. Pour into a martini glass, and garnish with a lime wheel.

2 oz vodka

1 oz apple schnapps

1 oz lime juice

4 oz crushed ice

Garnish:

lime wheel

SAPPHIRE ICE

Combine all ingredients in a blender, and blend until slushy. Serve unadorned in a martini glass.

2 oz lemon vodka

1 oz blue curaçao

1 splash sweet and sour mix

4 oz crushed ice

STRAWBERRY BLONDE

Combine all ingredients in a blender, and blend until smooth and frothy. Pour into a martini glass, and garnish with a strawberry.

2 oz vodka

2 oz champagne

1 oz pineapple juice

3 strawberries

4 oz crushed ice

Garnish:

fresh strawberry

ARCTIC PINEAPPLE

Combine all ingredients in a blender, and blend until slushy. Pour into highball glasses, and garnish extravagantly. Serves 2.

4 oz vodka

4 oz pineapple juice

6 oz frozen mango juice concentrate

3 oz crushed pineapple

1 oz lime juice

8 oz crushed ice

FROSTY ALASKAN ORANGE (page 208)

LIQUEUR-BASED

COCKTAILS

Liqueurs are spirits flavored with sweeteners, fruits, or herbal additives. These flavorings may be incorporated by infusion, distillation, percolation, or maceration. The history of these spirits is long and fascinating. Much of the research and development over the centuries was accomplished by monks, whose famed monasteries have given their names to such liqueurs as Chartreuse and Bénédictine. Italians in particular produced many of the greatest liqueurs, including almond-apricot amaretto, anise-based sambuca, and cherry-flavored maraschino, but the French mastered the anisette liqueurs (think Pernod and Ricard, and their New Orleans cousin Herbsaint), and the Caribbean gave rise to orange cordials like curaçao and triple sec. Because of their often syrupy feel and indulgent sweetness, liqueurs and cordials are most at home in rich frozen dessert cocktails and layered confectionary drinks. They feature in classics such as the Grasshopper, Bushwacker, and Barbara cocktails.

CAFFEINE ATTACK

Combine both ingredients in a blender, and blend until smooth. Pour into champagne coupes, and garnish with ground cinnamon or nutmeg. Serves 2.

1½ oz coffee liqueur

2 scoops coffee
  ice cream

Garnish:

cinnamon or nutmeg

COFFEE CREAM

Combine all ingredients in a blender, and blend briefly. Pour into a martini glass, and top with whipped cream.

2 oz coffee liqueur

2 oz heavy cream

2 oz crushed ice

Garnish:

whipped cream

PURE ECSTASY

Combine all ingredients in a blender, and blend briefly. Pour into a brandy snifter, and top with whipped cream and coffee beans.

2 oz coffee liqueur

4 oz Irish cream liqueur

1 oz vodka

4 oz crushed ice

Garnish:

whipped cream

coffee beans

FROZEN BLACK IRISH

Combine all ingredients in a blender, and blend until smooth. Serve in a footed goblet.

1½ oz coffee liqueur

1 oz Irish cream liqueur

½ oz vodka

1 scoop vanilla ice cream

4 oz crushed ice

OPPOSITE: Cocktails made from coffee-flavored liqueurs, such as Kahlúa, Starbucks Coffee Liqueur, and Tia Maria, make perfect after-dinner drinks.

BELOW: Frozen Black Irish is a perfect cocktail to take the place of hot Irish coffee during the sultry summer months.

155

PENSACOLA BUSHWACKER

Combine all ingredients in a blender, and blend until smooth. Pour into a hurricane glass, and garnish with a maraschino cherry.

2 oz coffee liqueur

1 oz black rum

1 oz crème de cacao

4 oz cream of coconut

4 oz half-and-half

1 scoop vanilla ice cream

8 oz crushed ice

Garnish:

maraschino cherry

LEFT: Pensacola Bushwacker. This drink has become so popular that it has its own celebration—the annual Bushwacker Festival—which has been held in Pensacola Beach, Florida, since 1986.

OPPOSITE: Bushwacker. This tropical coffee concoction, with a taste reminiscent of a creamy mocha Piña Colada, was first served in Florida in the mid 1970s.

BUSHWACKER

Combine all ingredients in a blender, and blend until smooth. Pour into a highball glass. Top with whipped cream and chocolate shavings.

1 oz coffee liqueur

½ oz dark rum

½ oz dark crème de cacao

2 oz cream of coconut

2 oz milk

6 oz crushed ice

Garnish:

whipped cream

chocolate shavings

COCONUT COFFEE

Combine all ingredients in a blender, and blend until smooth. Pour into a wine glass, and garnish with flaked coconut.

3 oz coffee liqueur

1½ oz cream of coconut

½ cup half-and-half

4 oz crushed ice

Garnish:

flaked coconut

COKAHLÚALICIOUS

Combine all ingredients in a blender, and
blend until smooth. Serve in a martini glass.

2 oz Kahlúa

2 oz coconut liqueur

4 oz crushed ice

HUMMINGBIRD

Combine all the ingredients in a blender, and blend until smooth. Pour into an old-fashioned glass, and garnish with whipped cream and a fresh strawberry.

1 oz coffee liqueur

1 oz rum cream liqueur

1 oz milk

½ oz strawberry syrup

½ medium banana

4 oz crushed ice

Garnish:

whipped cream

fresh strawberry

HUMMER

Combine coffee liqueur, rum, and one scoop of the ice cream in a blender, and blend until smooth. Pour into a margarita glass, and float the remaining ice cream on top.

1 oz coffee liqueur

1 oz light rum

2 scoops vanilla ice cream

COUNTRY CREAM

Combine all ingredients in a blender, and blend until smooth. Serve in a highball glass, and garnish with raspberries and a sprig of mint.

1 oz coffee liqueur

1 oz pear liqueur

½ oz Campari

¼ oz raspberry liqueur

3 tbsp vanilla ice cream

4 oz crushed ice

Garnish:

fresh raspberries

sprig of mint

CREAMY ALMOND COFFEE

Combine all ingredients in a blender, and blend until smooth. Serve in a highball glass, and garnish with grated chocolate.

2 oz coffee liqueur

3 oz Irish cream

2 oz amaretto

2 scoops vanilla ice cream

Garnish:

grated chocolate

163

LITTLE BROTHER

Combine all ingredients in a blender, and blend until smooth. Pour into a champagne coupe, and garnish with ground cinnamon.

2 oz coffee liqueur

1 oz vodka

1 scoop vanilla ice cream

1 tsp vanilla extract

Garnish:

ground cinnamon

MEXICAN MUDSLIDE

Combine all ingredients except the chocolate syrup and the ice cubes in a blender, and blend until smooth. Fill a hurricane glass with ice cubes, and then drizzle the chocolate syrup down the inside. Pour the mixture over the ice, and serve.

1 oz coffee liqueur

1 oz amaretto

1 scoop vanilla ice cream

1 oz chocolate syrup

ice cubes

165

CARAMEL NUT

Combine all ingredients except the caramel sauce in a blender, and blend until creamy. Swirl caramel sauce around the inside of a martini glass, and pour in mixture.

1 oz caramel liqueur

1 oz crème de cacao

1 scoop vanilla ice cream

1½ oz caramel sauce

NUT CRUSHER

Combine all ingredients in a blender, and blend until smooth. Pour into a champagne coupe, and sprinkle with grated hazelnuts, walnuts, or pecans.

1½ oz hazelnut liqueur

½ oz chocolate syrup

1 tbsp vanilla ice cream

4 oz crushed ice

Garnish:

grated nuts

BRAZILIAN MONK

Combine all ingredients in a blender, and blend until frothy. Pour into a wine glass, and garnish with bing cherries.

1 oz Frangelico hazelnut liqueur

1 oz coffee liqueur

1 oz crème de cacao

½ oz dry sherry

1 scoop vanilla ice cream

Garnish:

bing cherries

ORANGE MONK

Combine all ingredients in a blender, and blend until smooth. Pour into a brandy snifter, and garnish with an orange wedge.

1 oz Frangelico
  hazelnut liqueur

1 oz coffee liqueur

½ oz Irish cream liqueur

½ oz Grand Marnier

1 oz light cream

Garnish:

orange wedge

CRÈME BRÛLÉE MARTINI

Pour the Frangelico into the bottom of a martini glass, and then combine all other ingredients in a blender, and blend until smooth. Carefully layer the mixture over the Frangelico, and sprinkle brown sugar on top.

- 1 oz Frangelico hazelnut liqueur
- 1 oz vanilla vodka
- ½ oz butterscotch schnapps
- ½ oz heavy cream

Garnish:

brown sugar

MAPLE WALNUT

Coarsely grate five of the walnuts, reserving
two for the garnish, and then combine all
ingredients in a blender. Blend until creamy.
Pour into a martini glass, and garnish with
the reserved walnuts.

1½ oz hazelnut liqueur

3 tbsp vanilla ice cream

2 tbsp maple syrup

7 walnuts

TOASTED ALMOND

Combine all ingredients in a blender, and blend briefly until frothy. Pour into a chilled bolo grande glass, and garnish with a sprinkle of ground nutmeg.

¾ oz amaretto

¾ oz Kahlúa

2 oz heavy cream

Garnish:
ground nutmeg

BURNT ALMOND

Combine all ingredients in a blender, and blend briefly. Pour into a martini glass, and garnish with whole almonds.

1½ oz amaretto

1 oz Irish cream liqueur

½ oz vanilla vodka

1 oz cream

Garnish:

whole almonds

AMARETTO SUNRISE CRUSH

Rim a large martini glass with brown sugar, and then combine all ingredients except the lemon juice in a blender. Blend until smooth. Pour into the sugar-rimmed glass, and add the lemon juice.

1½ oz amaretto

¾ oz grenadine

4 oz orange juice

1 tsp lemon juice

4 oz crushed ice

Garnish:

2 tbsp brown sugar

OPPOSITE: Amaretto Sunrise Crush combines the nutty taste of almond-flavored liqueur with the bright tang of citrus fruit.

LEFT: Deep amber amaretto imparts a delicately bittersweet almond flavor to cocktails, but most brands of this liqueur contain no almonds—or any nuts at all. Instead, the flavor comes from the oil of apricot kernels.

BELOW: Apricot with kernel. When dry, these hard stones closely resemble almonds in look and taste.

TROLLEY CAR

Combine all ingredients, reserving one
strawberry for the garnish, in a blender.
Blend until smooth. Sieve into a wine glass
to remove any seeds, and garnish with the
reserved strawberry.

1¼ oz amaretto

6 fresh strawberries

2 scoops vanilla
   ice cream

CANADA DREAM

Combine all ingredients in a blender, and blend until smooth. Pour into a cocktail glass, and dust with cinnamon or nutmeg.

1 oz amaretto

1 oz apricot brandy

3 oz orange juice

2 oz crushed ice

Garnish:

cinnamon or nutmeg

Brute. The nutlike flavor of amaretto combines especially well with ice cream and chocolate.

BRUTE

Combine all ingredients in a blender, and blend until smooth and thick. Pour into a soda glass, and garnish with chopped almonds and chocolate syrup.

1 oz amaretto

1 oz dark crème de cacao

1 scoop vanilla ice cream

4 oz crushed ice

Garnish:

chopped almonds

chocolate syrup

ALASKAN KODIAK

Combine all ingredients in a blender, and blend until smooth. Pour into a highball glass, and embellish this cocktail with an extreme garnish.

1½ oz amaretto

1 oz hazelnut liqueur

1 oz cocoa cream

1 oz chocolate syrup

1 scoop chocolate
   ice cream

FRIESIAN

Combine all ingredients in a blender, and blend until smooth and thick. Pour into a collins glass, and garnish with a cheerful maraschino cherry.

1 oz amaretto

1 oz hazelnut liqueur

3 tbsp vanilla ice cream

1 tsp chocolate syrup

4 oz crushed ice

Garnish:

maraschino cherry

WHITE DOVE

Combine all ingredients except the chocolate syrup in a blender, and blend until smooth. Drizzle chocolate syrup along the insides of a brandy snifter, and pour in mixture. Top with whipped cream.

¾ oz amaretto

¾ oz white crème
   de cacao

2 scoops vanilla
   ice cream

1 oz chocolate syrup

Garnish:

whipped cream

BARBARA

Combine all ingredients in a blender, and blend briefly. Pour into a martini glass, and sprinkle grated chocolate on top.

½ oz white crème de cacao

1 oz vodka

½ oz heavy cream

Garnish:

grated chocolate

DULCE DE LECHE MARTINI

Combine all ingredients in a blender, and blend until smooth. Pour into a cocktail glass, and top with ground cinnamon.

¾ oz dark crème de cacao

1 oz rum

½ oz sweetened condensed milk

2 oz crushed ice

Garnish:

ground cinnamon

181

DARK DECADENCE

Combine all ingredients in a blender, and blend until smooth and silky. Pour into a cocktail glass, and garnish with cinnamon quills and chocolate shavings.

¾ oz dark crème de cacao

¾ oz coffee liqueur

¾ oz cinnamon schnapps

¾ oz 151-proof rum

¾ oz triple sec

3 scoops dark chocolate ice cream

Garnish:

cinnamon quills

chocolate shavings

CHOCOLATE ORANGE CREAM

Rim a martini glass with cocoa powder, and then combine the chocolate and Irish cream liqueurs in a blender with the crushed ice. Blend until smooth. Pour into the cocoa-rimmed glass, and top off with Grand Marnier. Garnish with an orange twist.

1½ oz chocolate liqueur
1 oz Irish cream liqueur
¾ oz Grand Marnier
4 oz crushed ice

Garnish:
2 tbsp cocoa powder
orange twist

CHERRY CHOCOLATE FREEZE

Combine all ingredients in a blender with crushed ice, and blend until smooth. Pour into a margarita glass, and garnish with a maraschino cherry.

1 oz dark crème de cacao

1 oz cherry brandy

½ oz chocolate syrup

2 tbsp vanilla ice cream

4 oz crushed ice

Garnish:

maraschino cherry

SHERRY FLIP

Pour all ingredients into a cocktail shaker, and shake until thoroughly chilled and frothy. Pour into a sour glass, and dust with ground nutmeg.

¼ oz light crème de cacao

1½ oz medium sherry

½ oz light cream

1 tsp superfine sugar

1 small whole egg

2 oz crushed ice

Garnish:

ground nutmeg

LIQUID COURAGE

Combine all ingredients in a blender, and blend until smooth. Pour into pilsner glasses, and garnish each with a dusting of cocoa powder. Serves 4.

10 oz white crème de cacao

6 oz vodka

6 oz light rum

16 oz milk

6 scoops vanilla ice cream

Garnish:

cocoa powder

DARK 'N' FLUFFY

Rim a martini glass with colored sugar, and then combine all ingredients in a blender, and blend until smooth. Pour mixture into a martini glass, float the marshmallow creme on top, and then finish with grated orange and lime zest.

2 oz Godiva dark chocolate liqueur

2 oz Smirnoff Fluffed Marshmallow vodka

1 oz heavy cream

Garnish:

2 tbsp colored sugar

marshmallow creme

orange and lime zest

IRISH DREAM

Combine all ingredients in a blender, and blend until smooth and creamy. Pour into a pint glass, and top with whipped cream and chocolate chips.

¾ oz dark crème de cacao

½ oz Irish cream liqueur

½ oz hazelnut liqueur

1 scoop vanilla ice cream

8 oz crushed ice

Garnish:

whipped cream

chocolate chips

TALBOT'S DREAM

Combine all ingredients in a blender, and blend until smooth. Pour into a cocktail glass, and sprinkle grated chocolate on top.

3 oz Godiva white chocolate liqueur

2 oz Irish cream liqueur

4 oz crushed ice

Garnish:

grated chocolate

PINK SQUIRREL

Combine all ingredients in a blender, and blend until smooth. Serve in a martini glass.

¾ oz white crème de cacao

¾ oz crème de noyaux

½ oz vodka

1 oz heavy cream

3 oz crushed ice

SEXY BLUE-EYED BOY

Rim a chilled parfait glass with blue-colored sugar or coconut flakes. Combine all ingredients in a blender, and blend until smooth. Pour into the rimmed glass, and top with whipped cream.

1 oz crème de cacao

1 oz blue curaçao

1 oz rum cream liqueur

1 oz vodka

1 scoop vanilla ice cream

2 oz crushed ice

Garnish:

3 tbsp colored sugar or coconut flakes

191

MOCHA MONKEY

Peel and slice the banana, and then combine all ingredients except the chocolate syrup in a blender. Blend until creamy. Swirl chocolate syrup around the inside of a hurricane glass, and pour in mixture. Top with whipped cream.

1½ oz Baileys Irish Cream

1 oz coffee liqueur

1 scoop vanilla ice cream

1 banana

2 tbsp chocolate syrup

Garnish:

whipped cream

IRISH JIG

Combine all ingredients in a blender, and blend until smooth. Pour into a hurricane glass, and top with the whipped cream.

1½ oz Irish cream liqueur

2 scoops vanilla ice cream

2 oz chocolate syrup

Garnish:

whipped cream

WHITE NILE

Combine all ingredients in a blender, and blend until smooth. Pour into a cocktail glass, and serve with a simple garnish.

1½ oz Amarula cream liqueur

1¼ oz Cointreau

1¼ oz dark crème de cacao

KISH WACKER

Combine all ingredients in a blender, and blend until smooth. Pour into a martini glass, and garnish with a sprig of mint.

1 oz Irish cream liqueur

½ oz crème de cacao

¼ oz coffee liqueur

½ oz vodka

4 oz crushed ice

Garnish:

sprig of mint

Mocha Monkey. Cream liqueurs are made from dairy cream that has been combined with a strong liquor and other ingredients. Baileys Irish Cream uses Irish whiskey. Other brands use Scotch whisky, rum, and vodka. Amarula is a South African cream liqueur that uses fermented marula fruits.

AFRICAN BREW

Combine all ingredients in a blender, and blend until smooth. Pour into a hurricane glass. This fanciful cocktail calls for a flamboyant garnish.

1½ oz Amarula cream liqueur

1 scoop chocolate ice cream

1 small banana

1 tsp cocoa powder

4 oz crushed ice

SWINGING SAFARI

Combine all ingredients in a blender, and blend until smooth. Pour into a martini glass, and garnish with a maraschino cherry.

1½ oz Amarula cream liqueur

1¼ oz Cointreau

½ oz vodka

4 oz crushed ice

Garnish:
maraschino cherry

AMARULA SUNSET

Combine all ingredients in a blender, and blend until smooth. Pour into a cocktail glass, and garnish with a fresh strawberry.

1½ oz Amarula cream liqueur

1 scoop vanilla ice cream

2 tsp strawberry puree

Garnish:

fresh strawberry

CHOCO-MINT AMARULA CREAM

Combine all ingredients except the heavy cream in a blender, and blend until smooth. Pour into a martini glass, and swirl in the cream. Top with a mint leaf.

1½ oz Amarula cream liqueur

½ oz white crème de menthe

2 tbsp chocolate ice cream

1 tbsp heavy cream

Garnish:

mint leaf

ICE CREAM GENIUS

Combine all ingredients in a blender, and blend until smooth. Pour into a margarita glass, and garnish with an orange wheel.

2 oz amaretto

4 oz orange juice

2 scoops vanilla
   ice cream

Garnish:
orange wheel

ICE CREAM FLIP

Combine all ingredients in a blender, and blend until smooth. Pour into a champagne coupe, and sprinkle with ground nutmeg.

1 oz maraschino liqueur

1½ oz triple sec

1 scoop vanilla ice cream

1 whole egg

4 oz crushed ice

Garnish:
ground nutmeg

GORILLA MILK

Combine all ingredients in a blender, and blend until smooth. Pour into a large wine glass, and garnish with a slice of banana.

1 oz coffee liqueur

¾ oz amaretto

¾ oz banana schnapps

2 scoops vanilla ice cream

Garnish:
sliced banana

COCOA MINT DREAM

Combine all ingredients in a blender, and blend until smooth. Pour into a cocktail glass, and garnish with a sprig of mint and a sprinkle of cocoa powder.

1 oz white crème de cacao

1 oz green crème
   de menthe

1 scoop mint ice cream

Garnish:
sprig of mint

cocoa powder

Cocoa Mint Dream. Ice cream—based cocktails are delicious alternatives to traditional desserts.

GOLDEN CADILLAC

Combine all ingredients in a blender, and blend until smooth. Pour into a martini glass, and serve with an elegant garnish.

1 oz Galliano
   herbal liqueur

2 oz white crème
   de cacao

1 oz light cream

4 oz crushed ice

GOLDEN DREAM

Combine all ingredients in a blender, and blend until smooth. Pour into martini glasses. Serves 2 to 3.

2 oz Galliano herbal liqueur

1 oz white crème de cacao

½ oz triple sec

3 oz orange juice

3 oz light cream

4 oz crushed ice

FROZEN GRASSHOPPER

Combine all the ingredients in a blender, and blend briefly, just until smooth. Serve in a martini glass with a simple garnish.

1½ oz green crème de menthe

1½ oz white crème de cacao

1 scoop vanilla ice cream

LEFT: Crème de menthe is a sweet mint-flavored liqueur that comes in green and clear varieties. The "crème" in the name of a liqueur does not refer to any cream content, but rather to high sugar content.

OPPOSITE: The Frozen Grasshopper. The classic Grasshopper is said to have first been served in New Orlean's French Quarter in the 1920s, and it became a hit with the cocktail set of the 1950s and 1960s. The original contains equal parts green crème de menthe, white crème de cacao, and heavy cream.

BELOW: The Frozen Grasshopper, which uses ice cream rather than fresh cream, is a natural twist on the original.

PEPPERMINT PENGUIN

Combine all ingredients in a blender, and blend until smooth. Pour into a highball glass, and garnish with the crumbled chocolate sandwich cookies.

½ oz green crème de menthe

½ oz chocolate mint liqueur

3 oz light cream

4 oz crushed ice

Garnish:

3 chocolate sandwich cookies, crumbled

LICORICE MIST

Combine all ingredients in a blender, and blend until smooth. Pour into a champagne flute, and garnish with a lime wheel and a sprig of elderflower.

1¼ oz sambuca

½ oz coconut liqueur

2 oz light cream

2 oz crushed ice

Garnish:

fresh lime

sprig of elderflower

Jäger Vacation. Look beyond the usual when choosing liqueurs for your frozen cocktails. Herbal liqueurs, such as the German Jägermeister with its blend of 56 herbs and spices, and Strega—an Italian liqueur made from 70 herbs, including mint and fennel—add complexity to their taste.

JÄGER VACATION

Combine all ingredients in a blender, and blend until smooth. Pour into a hurricane glass, and lavishly decorate with a tropical-inspired garnish.

1½ oz Jägermeister herbal liqueur

3 tbsp cream of coconut

2 oz pineapple juice

4 oz crushed ice

GLACIERMEISTER

Combine all ingredients in a blender, and blend until smooth and creamy. Pour mixture into a margarita glass, and garnish with a sprig of mint.

1½ oz Jägermeister herbal liqueur

2 scoops vanilla ice cream

1½ oz milk

2 oz crushed ice

Garnish:
sprig of mint

BRUJA MEXICANA

Combine the Strega and Agavero in a blender with the crushed ice, and blend until frothy. Pour into a highball glass, add the sugar syrup, and top up with the soda water.

1½ oz Strega herbal liqueur

1 oz Agavero tequila liqueur

6 oz soda water

1 tsp sugar syrup

4 oz crushed ice

CALM VOYAGE

Combine all ingredients in a blender, and blend until light and frothy. Pour into a champagne flute, and serve unadorned.

½ oz Strega herbal liqueur

½ oz light rum

1 tbsp passion fruit syrup

1 tsp lemon juice

½ oz egg white

4 oz crushed ice

FROSTY ALASKAN ORANGE

Combine all the ingredients in a blender, and blend until smooth. Pour into a hurricane glass, and garnish extravagantly.

2 oz orange liqueur

¾ oz brandy

4 tbsp vanilla
   ice cream

4 oz crushed ice

ICY ORANGE

Combine all the ingredients in a blender, and blend until smooth. Pour into a hurricane glass, and garnish with a maraschino cherry and an orange twist.

4 oz orange liqueur

16 oz orange juice

12 oz lemon-lime soda

1 cubed mango

5 sliced strawberries

juice of ½ lemon

4 oz crushed ice

Garnish:

orange twist

maraschino cherry

ICEBERG IN RADIOACTIVE WATER

Combine all ingredients in a blender, and blend until smooth. Pour into margarita glasses, and drop a scoop of ice cream into each immediately before serving. Serves 2.

3 oz melon liqueur

1 oz coconut rum

1 oz banana liqueur

8 oz pineapple juice

2 scoops vanilla ice cream

KORI'S SATURDAY NIGHT SPECIAL

Combine all the ingredients in a blender, and blend until smooth. Pour into a hurricane glass, and serve with a straw.

1 oz banana liqueur

1 oz coconut rum

½ oz dark rum

1 scoop vanilla ice cream

NUTTY PUMPKIN PIE

Combine all ingredients in a blender, and blend until smooth. Pour mixture into a martini glass, and garnish with a dusting of pumpkin pie spice.

1½ oz pumpkin
    spice liqueur

1 oz Baileys Irish Cream

1 oz light cream

½ oz vanilla vodka

½ oz amaretto

2 oz crushed ice

Garnish:

pumpkin pie spice

CHERRY PIE

Rim a chilled martini glass with a mixture of graham cracker crumbs and powdered sugar. Mix the cherry pie liqueur and the vanilla vodka in a cocktail shaker filled with ice cubes. Shake vigorously, and then strain into the rimmed glass. Drop the cherries into the glass, and serve.

1½ oz cherry pie liqueur

3 oz vanilla vodka

ice cubes

Garnish:

2 tbsp graham
   cracker crumbs

1 tbsp powdered sugar

2 bing cherries

MOCHA BANANA

Combine all ingredients in a blender, and blend until smooth and thick. Pour into a double cocktail glass, and garnish with grated chocolate.

1 oz crème de bananes

1 oz crème de cacao

1 oz coffee liqueur

2 scoops vanilla ice cream

4 oz crushed ice

Garnish:

grated chocolate

BANANA KISS

Combine all ingredients in a blender, and blend until smooth. Pour into a hurricane glass, and garnish with sliced banana.

3 oz crème de bananes

1 oz crème de cacao

¾ oz cream of coconut

2 oz milk

1½ oz heavy cream

4 oz crushed ice

Garnish:

sliced banana

215

SNOWFLAKE

Combine all ingredients except the lemon-lime soda in a blender, and blend until smooth. Pour into a highball glass, top off with soda, and garnish with a slice of pear.

1½ oz pear liqueur

3 oz milk

3 oz lemon-lime soda

3 oz crushed ice

Garnish:

fresh pear

RASPBERRY LIQUEUR DAIQUIRI

Combine all ingredients, reserving one of the raspberries for the garnish, in a blender, and blend until smooth. Pour into a martini glass, and garnish with a wedge of lime and the reserved raspberry.

¾ oz raspberry liqueur

¾ oz light rum

½ oz lime juice

7 whole raspberries

1 tsp powdered sugar

4 oz crushed ice

Garnish:

lime wedge

MIDORI CHAN

Combine all ingredients in a blender, and blend until smooth. Pour into a highball glass, and garnish with melon balls and a sprig of mint.

1½ oz Midori melon liqueur

1 oz light rum

1 oz piña colada mix

2 slices canned pineapple

4 oz crushed ice

Garnish:

fresh melon balls

sprig of mint

FROZEN MIDORI SOUR

Combine all the ingredients in a blender, and blend until chilled. Serve in a highball glass with a melon ball garnish.

2 oz Midori melon liqueur

6 oz sweet and sour mix

½ tsp sugar

4 oz crushed ice

Garnish:
fresh melon balls

LEMON CHEESECAKE

Rim a chilled martini glass with a mixture of graham cracker crumbs and powdered sugar. Combine all ingredients in a blender, and blend until smooth. Pour into the rimmed glass, and garnish with a lemon wedge.

1 oz limoncello liqueur

¾ oz hazelnut liqueur

¾ oz pinot grigio

1 tsp gingerbread syrup

1 tsp cinnamon syrup

¾ oz cream

¾ oz milk

2 oz crushed ice

Garnish:

2 tbsp graham cracker crumbs

1 tbsp powdered sugar

lemon wedge

LIMONCELLO SLUSH

Prepare lemon syrup by mixing hot water, sugar, and lemon juice. When the syrup is cool, combine it with the rest of the ingredients in a blender, and blend until slushy. Pour into a highball glass, and garnish with a lemon wheel.

1 oz limoncello liqueur

1 oz vodka

4 oz lemonade

4 tsp lemon juice

2 oz hot water

4 tbsp sugar

8 oz crushed ice

Garnish:

lemon wheel

GREEN WHALE

Rim a chilled hurricane glass with coarse salt, and then combine all ingredients in a blender. Blend until smooth. Pour into the salt-rimmed glass, and garnish with an orange wheel.

1½ oz blue curaçao

½ oz vodka

2 oz pineapple juice

4 oz orange juice

1 tsp sugar

4 oz crushed ice

Garnish:

2 tbsp coarse salt

orange wheel

GREEN COW

Combine all the ingredients except the lemon-lime soda in a blender, and blend until smooth. Pour into a pilsner glass, add the soda, and serve.

3 oz Pisang Ambon liqueur

1½ oz vodka

3 oz milk

2 oz lemon-lime soda

4 oz crushed ice

BRANDY SLUSH (page 230)

BRANDY, WHISKEY & GIN-BASED

COCKTAILS

Brandy, whiskey, and gin feature in many of the most revered traditional drinks, including the Brandy Alexander. Brandy is distilled from grapes, and it is traditionally associated with France, where the great spirits of cognac, armagnac, and calvados (the finest apple brandy) have long and glorious histories. Whiskey (or whisky, depending on the country it comes from) is available in an even wider variety, from bourbon and rye to Scotch, Canadian, and even superb spirits from Japan and India. Gin, a clear spirit flavored with juniper berries, originated in medieval times in what is now the Netherlands, but gained enormous popularity in England in the late seventeenth century. It has since become the foundation of such mainstays as the martini. In recent years boutique gins have proliferated, many of which are fantastic bases for frozen cocktails.

ICED COFFEE L'ORANGE

Combine cool fresh-brewed coffee in a
blender with the brandy and orange liqueur.
Add a dash of cream, if desired, and blend
until frothy. Pour into a champagne coupe,
and float espresso beans on top.

1 oz brandy

1 oz orange liqueur

1 oz coffee, chilled

1 dash cream

Garnish:
espresso beans

226

FROZEN BRANDY AND RUM

Combine all ingredients in a blender, and blend briefly at low speed. Pour into a chilled old-fashioned glass, and garnish with autumn spices, such as cinnamon sticks and star anise.

1½ oz brandy

1 oz light rum

1 tbsp lemon juice

1 tsp powdered sugar

1 egg white

2 oz crushed ice

Garnish:

cinnamon stick

star anise

BRANDY ALEXANDER

Combine all ingredients in a blender, and blend until smooth. Pour into a cocktail glass, and garnish with ground nutmeg.

1 oz cognac brandy

½ oz crème de cacao

1 scoop vanilla ice cream

3 oz crushed ice

Garnish:

ground nutmeg

LEFT: Brandy Alexanders are traditionally made with cognac, an aged brandy from the region around Cognac, France. Famous brands include Courvoisier, Martell, Hennessy, and Rémy Martin.

BELOW AND OPPOSITE: Brandy Alexander. This cocktail began as a variation of the Alexander, a gin-based drink. The popularity of the brandy version soon eclipsed that of the original.

BRANDY SLUSH

Combine all the ingredients in a blender, and blend until slushy. Pour into a highball glass, and serve with a simple garnish.

1½ oz brandy

1 oz rum

1 tbsp lemon juice

1 tsp powdered sugar

1 egg

6 oz crushed ice

COCONUT BRANDY BOWL

Slice the coconuts in half, and pour the milk into a bowl. Gouge out the coconut flesh, and store it for another use. Strain the coconut milk into a blender, and then add the remaining ingredients. Blend at high speed until thoroughly chilled. Pour the contents into two of the open coconut shells, stick in straws, and garnish extravagantly. Serves 2.

3 oz brandy

1½ oz banana liqueur

milk of 2 large coconuts

4 oz crushed ice

FROZEN BARCELONA

Combine all ingredients in a blender, and blend until smooth. Pour into an iced tea glass, and garnish with fresh fruit.

¾ oz Spanish brandy

¾ oz dry sherry

¾ oz orange liqueur

¾ oz orange juice

¾ oz heavy cream

1 oz simple syrup

4 oz crushed ice

CRICKETS

Combine all the ingredients in a blender, and blend until smooth. Pour into a pilsner glass, and serve with a straw.

1½ oz peach brandy

3 oz white crème de cacao

4 oz chopped fresh peaches

2 scoops vanilla ice cream

4 oz crushed ice

PORTO FLIP

Pour all ingredients into a cocktail shaker, and shake until thoroughly chilled. Strain into a cordial glass, and dust with nutmeg.

¼ oz brandy

1½ oz ruby port

¾ oz cream

½ tsp powdered sugar

1 egg yolk

Garnish:

ground nutmeg

LEFT AND OPPOSITE: Porto Flip. "Flips" were a popular form of drink up until the nineteenth century, and these cocktails are now making a comeback.

BELOW: Flips get their rich, silky texture from the addition of eggs, often just the yolks. When using egg yolks, shake vigorously to make sure that they fully emulsify. To avoid the risk of salmonella, use pasteurized eggs, which are now becoming more widely available. The pasteurization process kills any harmful bacteria in the egg.

CAPE SNOW

Combine all ingredients in a blender, and blend until smooth. Pour into a parfait glass, garnish with an orange wedge, and serve.

1 oz brandy

1 oz Van Der Hum liqueur

1 scoop vanilla ice cream

Garnish:

orange wedge

PISCO SOUR

Combine the sugar and lime juice until the sugar is dissolved. Pour into a blender, and add the brandy, egg white, and crushed ice. Blend until frothy. Pour into an old-fashioned glass, and add a few drops of bitters.

2 oz pisco brandy

1 tbsp egg white

2 tbsp sugar

juice of ½ lime

1 dash Angostura bitters

2 oz crushed ice

PISCO-RITA

Combine all ingredients in a blender, and blend at high speed until frothy. Pour into a margarita glass, and serve unadorned.

6 oz pisco brandy

6 oz frozen limeade

3 oz triple sec

4 oz crushed ice

ABOVE: Pisco Sour (front) and Pisco-Rita. Pisco is an amber-colored brandy from Peru and Chile.

CHILLY IRISHMAN

Combine ingredients in a blender, adding the crushed ice until smooth. Pour into parfait glasses. Serves 2.

1 oz Irish whiskey

½ oz Kahlúa

½ oz Baileys Irish Cream

3 oz espresso, chilled

1 scoop vanilla ice cream

½ tsp simple syrup

32 oz crushed ice

IRISH FRUIT FLY

Drain the syrup from the fruit cocktail, and then combine all ingredients in a blender. Blend at high speed until thick and slushy. Pour into a highball glass, and garnish with a cinnamon stick.

1 oz Irish whiskey

8½-oz can fruit cocktail

1 tbsp ground cinnamon

4 oz crushed ice

Garnish:

cinnamon stick

239

FROZEN GAEL

Combine all ingredients in a blender, and blend briefly at low speed. Pour into an old-fashioned glass, and garnish with a dusting of ground nutmeg.

1 oz Scotch whisky

1 oz Baileys Irish Cream

2 tbsp vanilla ice cream

1 tbsp crushed ice

Garnish:

ground nutmeg

PINK PANTIES

Combine all ingredients in a blender, and blend until smooth. Pour into a highball glass, and garnish with a lemon wheel and a fresh strawberry.

8 oz Canadian Mist whisky

6 oz frozen pink lemonade concentrate

8 oz water

4 oz frozen whipped topping

Garnish:

fresh strawberry

lemon wheel

FROZEN WHISKEY SOUR

Combine all ingredients in a blender, and blend until slushy. Pour into chilled old-fashioned glasses, and garnish each with a maraschino cherry. Serves 4.

4 oz whiskey

3 oz frozen lemonade concentrate

3 oz frozen orange juice concentrate

4 oz grenadine

½ cup superfine sugar

8 oz crushed ice

Garnish:
maraschino cherries

DEER KILLER

Combine all ingredients except the butterscotch schnapps in a large blender, and blend until frothy. Pour contents into mason jars, and splash a bit of butterscotch schnapps into each. Garnish with ground cinnamon and cinnamon sticks. Drizzle each drink with the hot melting butter right before you serve. Serves 5.

5 oz bourbon whiskey

3 oz whiskey

8 oz cinnamon schnapps

15 oz Jägermeister herbal liqueur

1 oz vodka

2 tbsp Tabasco sauce

5 splashes butterscotch schnapps

4 oz crushed ice

Garnish:

cinnamon

1 tbsp melted butter

243

FROZEN EGG NOG

Combine all ingredients in a large blender, and blend until smooth. Pour into cocktail glasses, and serve with a seasonal garnish. Serves 8 to 16.

6 oz bourbon whiskey

6 oz spiced rum

32 oz prepared egg nog

16 oz vanilla ice cream

KENTUCKY MORNING

Pour all ingredients into a cocktail shaker, and shake until thoroughly chilled and frothy. Pour into a cocktail glass, and dust with cinnamon.

2 oz bourbon whiskey

1 oz fresh-squeezed lemon juice

½ oz simple syrup

1 egg white

1 tsp apricot preserves

2 oz crushed ice

Garnish:

ground cinnamon

SLOE GIN FLIP

Pour all ingredients into a cocktail shaker, and shake until thoroughly chilled and frothy. Pour into a sour glass, and dust with ground nutmeg.

1½ oz sloe gin

1 tsp superfine sugar

1 small whole egg

2 oz crushed ice

Garnish:

ground nutmeg

VISITOR

Pour all ingredients into a cocktail shaker, and shake until thoroughly chilled and frothy. Pour unstrained into an ungarnished cocktail glass.

1 oz gin

1 oz crème de bananes

1 oz triple sec

1 oz egg white

1 splash orange juice

2 oz crushed ice

ABOVE: Silver Stallion Fizz. A fizz cocktail relies on the addition of carbonated club soda for its foamy texture.

SILVER STALLION FIZZ

Pour all ingredients except the club soda into a blender, and blend briefly, just until thoroughly chilled. Pour into a highball glass, and then fill the glass with club soda. Stir and serve.

2 oz gin

1 scoop vanilla ice cream

club soda

2 oz crushed ice

RAMOS GIN FIZZ

Pour all ingredients except the club soda into a cocktail shaker, and shake vigorously until thoroughly chilled. Pour into a chilled wine glass, fill the glass with club soda, and stir. Garnish with an orange wheel.

1½ oz gin

½ oz lime juice

½ oz lemon juice

1¼ oz simple syrup

2 oz light cream

1 egg white

¼ oz orange flower water

club soda

Garnish:
orange wheel

Ramos Gin Fizz. Also known as the New Orleans Fizz, this famed cocktail was created in the late 1800s by bar owner Henry C. Ramos at his Imperial Cabinet Saloon in the French Quarter.

PINK LADY

Pour all ingredients into a cocktail shaker, and shake until chilled and creamy. Strain into a cocktail glass, and serve.

1½ oz gin

¼ oz grenadine

¾ oz simple syrup

1 oz heavy cream

2 oz crushed ice

ALEXANDER

Pour all ingredients into a cocktail shaker, and shake until chilled. Pour into a chilled champagne coupe, and dust with nutmeg.

1 oz gin

1 oz crème de cacao

2 oz heavy cream

2 oz crushed ice

Garnish:

ground nutmeg

FROZEN MONKEY GLAND

Combine all ingredients in a blender, and blend until slushy. Pour into a cocktail glass, and serve unadorned.

1½ oz gin

1½ oz fresh orange juice

1 tsp grenadine

1 tsp simple syrup

1 tsp absinthe

3 oz crushed ice

STRAWBERRY DAWN

Combine all ingredients in a blender, and blend until smooth. Pour into a cocktail glass, and top with a single fresh strawberry.

1 oz gin

1 oz cream of coconut

4 oz frozen strawberries

4 oz crushed ice

Garnish:

fresh strawberry

WHITE CARGO

Pour all ingredients into a cocktail shaker, and shake until thoroughly chilled. Pour into a martini glass, and serve.

2½ oz dry gin

¼ oz white wine

1 scoop vanilla ice cream

CLOVER CLUB

Pour all ingredients into a cocktail shaker, and shake until thoroughly chilled and frothy. Pour into a cocktail glass or a champagne coupe, and serve immediately.

1½ oz gin

¾ oz fresh lemon juice

2 tsp raspberry syrup

1 egg white

2 oz crushed ice

GOLDEN MARGARITA (page 265)

TEQUILA-BASED

COCKTAILS

Tequila, both loved and reviled as one of the world's more hangover-inducing spirits, is actually a variety of *mezcal*, the spirit distilled in Mexico from the agave plant. Tequila must come from the area around the town of Tequila in Jalisco province, and it must be distilled primarily from blue agave. As with many other spirits, tequilas are also categorized by the manner and duration of the aging they undergo; the five categories are *blanco* (also known as white or silver, and barely aged), *joven* (also called gold because of added color or blending with aged tequila), *reposado* (aged in wooden barrels for at least sixty days), *añejo* (aged in wooden barrels for at least a year), and *extra añejo* (aged in wooden barrels for at least three years). As with rum, the finest premium tequilas are made for sipping—white tequila usually serves as the base for a cocktail. Blending exceptionally well with fruit juice, tequila is the base for the classic margarita, as well as its myriad frozen variations.

FROZEN MARGARITA

Rim a margarita glass with coarse salt, and then combine all ingredients in a blender. Blend at high speed until slushy. Pour into the salt-rimmed glass, and garnish with a lime or lemon wheel.

1½ oz tequila

½ oz triple sec

1 oz lime juice

8 oz crushed ice

Garnish:

2 tbsp coarse salt

lime or lemon wheel

LEFT: *Blanco* tequilas, such as Patron Silver, are ultra-smooth tequilas that make perfect bases for frozen margaritas.

OPPOSITE: The Frozen Margarita—a simple but seductive summer cocktail.

BELOW: A glass rimmed with salt is a margarita essential. For best results, sprinkle a tablespoon or two of coarse salt onto a plate, rub the rim of the glass with a lemon or lime wedge, and then swirl it in the salt.

STRAWBERRY MARGARITA

Rim a margarita glass with coarse salt, and then combine all ingredients in a blender. Blend at high speed until slushy. Pour into the salt-rimmed glass, and garnish with a fresh strawberry.

3 oz tequila

1½ oz triple sec

4 oz strawberry margarita mix

Garnish:

2 tbsp coarse salt

fresh strawberry

STRAWBERRY MANGO MARGARITA

Rim four margarita glasses with coarse salt, and then combine all ingredients in a blender. Blend at high speed until slushy. Pour into the salt-rimmed glasses. To garnish, thread fresh strawberries with lemon and lime wedges on cocktail spears. Serves 4.

4 oz tequila

5 oz triple sec

12½ oz mango juice

12 oz fresh strawberries

4 oz crushed ice

Garnish:

2 tbsp coarse salt

fresh strawberry

lemon and lime wedges

FROZEN ROSE MARGARITA

Rim a martini glass with sugar, and then combine all ingredients in a blender. Blend until slushy. Pour into the sugar-rimmed glass, and garnish with rose petals.

1½ oz tequila

2 oz rose nectar

¾ oz Cointreau

1 oz lime juice

1 dash simple syrup

2 oz crushed ice

Garnish:

2 tbsp sugar

rose petals

GINGER-COCONUT MARGARITA

Rim a margarita glass with sugar, and then combine all ingredients in a blender. Blend at high speed until slushy. Pour into the sugar-rimmed glass, and garnish with sliced ginger and flaked coconut.

1½ oz tequila

½ oz ginger liqueur

2 tbsp cream of coconut

1 splash sour mix

1 splash orange juice

4 oz crushed ice

Garnish:

2 tbsp sugar

flaked coconut

sliced ginger

CREAMSICLE MARGARITA

Rim a margarita glass with sugar, and then combine all ingredients in a blender. Blend until thick and creamy. Pour into the sugar-rimmed glass, and garnish simply with a fresh orange wedge.

1¼ oz gold tequila

3 oz orange juice

1 oz sweet and sour mix

1 scoop vanilla ice cream

6 oz crushed ice

Garnish:

2 tbsp sugar

orange wedge

Frozen Rose Margarita. Swap sugar for the usual salt when rimming the glass for a sweet margarita.

CRANBERRY MARGARITA

Rim a margarita glass with coarse salt, and then combine all ingredients in a blender. Blend at high speed just until slushy. Pour mixture into the salt-rimmed glass, and garnish with a lime wedge.

1½ oz tequila

1 oz Rose's lime juice

1½ oz triple sec

1½ oz sweet and sour mix

2 oz cranberry juice

Garnish:

2 tbsp coarse salt

lime wedge

GOLDEN MARGARITA

Rim a margarita glass with coarse salt, and then combine all ingredients in a blender. Blend until slushy. Pour into the salt-rimmed glass, and garnish with a lemon wheel.

1½ oz gold tequila

½ oz orange liqueur

½ oz lime juice

3 oz sour mix

1 dash orange juice

4 oz crushed ice

Garnish:

2 tbsp coarse salt

lemon wheel

WHITECAP MARGARITA

Combine all ingredients in a blender, and
blend until slushy. Pour into a margarita
glass. Garnish extravagantly with exotic fruit.

2 oz white tequila

1 oz cream of coconut

½ oz lime juice

4 oz crushed ice

GUAVA JALAPEÑO MARGARITA

Place the whole jalapeños and the tequila in a small bowl. Cover, and set aside for a day. When the tequila is fully infused, discard the jalapeños. Rim four margarita glasses with Hawaiian pink salt. Combine the infused tequila with the other ingredients in a blender, and blend until slushy. Pour into the salt-rimmed glasses, and garnish with a slice of jalapeño. Serves 4.

2 jalapeño peppers, whole

4¼ oz tequila

2 oz Cointreau

4¼ oz fresh lime juice

4 oz guava juice

8 oz crushed ice

Garnish:

2 tbsp Hawaiian pink salt

slice of jalapeño

ULTIMATE BLUE MARGARITA

Rim a margarita glass with coarse salt, and then combine all ingredients in a blender. Blend at high speed until slushy. Pour into the salt-rimmed glass, and garnish with a lemon wheel.

3 oz tequila

1 oz blue curaçao

2 oz lime juice

4 oz crushed ice

Garnish:

2 tbsp coarse salt

lemon wheel

LEFT AND BELOW: The potent flavors of tequila-based cocktails often call for simple garnishes like lemon and lime wheels.

OPPOSITE: Both the Ultimate Blue Margarita (front) and the Ultimate Margarita should have the consistency of icy slush—the perfect refreshment for a hot night.

ULTIMATE MARGARITA

Rim a margarita glass with coarse salt, and then combine all ingredients in a blender. Blend at high speed until slushy. Pour into the salt-rimmed glass, and garnish with a lime wheel.

3 oz tequila

1 oz Cointreau

1 oz sweet and sour mix

juice of ¼ lime

4 oz crushed ice

Garnish:

2 tbsp coarse salt

lime wheel

POMEGRANATE MARGARITA

Rim a margarita glass with colored sugar, and then combine all ingredients in a blender. Blend at high speed until slushy. Pour into the salt-rimmed glass, and garnish with a lime wheel and pomegranate pips.

1 oz tequila

2 oz pomegranate liqueur

½ oz triple sec

juice of ¼ lime

1 dash simple syrup

4 oz crushed ice

Garnish:

2 tbsp colored sugar

fresh pomegranate pips

ALMOND MARGARITA

Rim a margarita glass with coarse salt, and then combine all ingredients in a blender. Blend until slushy. Pour into the salt-rimmed glass, and garnish with a lime wheel.

1 oz tequila

1 oz amaretto

1 oz fresh-squeezed
   lime juice

4 oz crushed Ice

Garnish:

2 tbsp coarse salt

lime wheel

WATERMELON MARGARITA

Cut up a watermelon, and remove all the seeds. Reserve several chunks to use as a garnish, and then liquefy in a blender until you have about 16 ounces. Add remaining ingredients, and blend until smooth. Pour into margarita glasses, and garnish with the reserved watermelon. Serves 2 to 4.

6 oz tequila

3 oz triple sec

16 oz seeded, pureed watermelon

juice of ½ lime

1 tbsp sugar

LEFT AND OPPOSITE: Watermelon Margaritas. Although cocktail purists may insist that a true margarita must feature a salt-rimmed glass, it is optional. Including coarse salt, however, enhances the flavor, with the salt bringing out the sweetness of the watermelon.

BELOW: The texture of watermelon works well in frozen drinks, but beware the seeds. Carefully remove both the black and white seeds before pureeing the fruit. For a less grainy texture, press watermelon puree through a fine-meshed strainer.

MEXICAN BLUEBERRY

Rim two martini glasses with colored sugar. Reserving several blueberries for the garnish, combine all ingredients in a blender. Blend at high speed until slushy. Pour into the salt-rimmed glasses, and garnish with the reserved blueberries. Serves 2.

4 oz tequila

2 oz orange liqueur

2 oz orange juice

2 cups fresh or frozen blueberries

6 oz frozen limeade concentrate

4 tbsp powdered sugar

16 oz crushed ice

Garnish:

4 tbsp colored sugar

TROPICAL FRUIT SLUSH

Combine all ingredients in a blender, and blend at high speed until slushy. Pour into margarita glasses, and garnish extravagantly. Serves 2.

4 oz tequila

6 oz frozen guava-passion-orange juice concentrate

4 tsp frozen limeade concentrate

4 tsp fresh lime juice

16 oz crushed ice

GREEN IGUANA

Rim a cocktail glass with coarse salt, and then combine all ingredients in a blender. Blend until chilled. Pour mixture into the salt-rimmed glass, and garnish simply with a lime wedge.

½ oz tequila

1 oz melon liqueur

2 oz sweet and sour mix

4 oz crushed ice

Garnish:

2 tbsp coarse salt

lime wedge

THE DANGEROUS DAVE

Rim four martini glasses with sugar, and then combine all ingredients in a blender. Blend at high speed until slushy. Pour into the sugar-rimmed glasses, and garnish each with fresh pineapple. Serves 4.

6 oz tequila

8 oz cream of coconut

8 oz pineapple juice

4 oz crushed ice

Garnish:

8 tbsp sugar

fresh pineapple

FROZEN MATADOR

Combine all ingredients in a blender, and blend at high speed until slushy. Pour into a champagne coupe or cocktail glass, and garnish with fresh pineapple.

1½ oz tequila

2 oz pineapple juice

1 tbsp lime juice

8 oz crushed ice

Garnish:

fresh pineapple

TEQUILA FROST

Combine all ingredients in a blender, and
blend until smooth. Pour into a parfait glass,
and garnish with an orange wedge.

1½ oz tequila

1¼ oz pineapple juice

1¼ oz grapefruit juice

½ oz honey

½ oz grenadine

4 tbsp vanilla ice cream

Garnish:

orange wedge

279

SPICED FRUIT PUNCH SLUSH (page 288)

SCHNAPPS -BASED

COCKTAILS

The word *schnapps* derives from a Low German word for "a mouthful"—a clear enough indicator of this spirit's traditional role as a quick, warming shot. In Germany, it refers to any strong spirit, but elsewhere you should keep in mind that schnapps might refer to either of two basic styles of spirit. The first is a Germanic one, clean and sharp like grappa and other spirits flavored with such fruits as cherry, apricot, or apple. The other kind is—for lack of a better term—American schnapps, best described as a liqueur or cordial. It is made from neutral grain spirits enhanced with a vast range of flavors, from fruit to herbs to candy, and thickened with sugar and glycerine for a more syrupy consistency. Schnapps come into their own in frozen cocktails, where their saccharine quality, balanced with sour ingredients, makes for a pleasingly sweet-and-tart effect. But be careful: schnapps are both more alcoholic than most liqueurs and more intensely flavorful, so they require careful measuring.

PEPPERMINT CREAM

Combine all ingredients in a blender, and blend until smooth. Pour into a highball glass, and top with whipped cream. Garnish with a sprig of mint.

½ oz peppermint schnapps

1 oz green crème de menthe

1 scoop vanilla ice cream

Garnish:

whipped cream

sprig of mint

PEPPERMINT MARSHMALLOW

Rim a martini glass with rainbow sprinkles. Combine all ingredients in a blender, and blend until smooth and creamy. Pour into the rimmed glass, and decorate with a candy cane and mini marshmallows.

1 oz peppermint schnapps

1 oz white crème de cacao

2 tbsp vanilla ice cream

1 tbsp marshmallow creme

Garnish:

2 tbsp rainbow sprinkles

candy cane

mini marshmallows

ICEBERG

Combine all ingredients in a blender, and blend until smooth. Pour into a frosted pilsner glass. Garnish with a sprig of mint and a cinnamon stick.

1 oz peppermint schnapps

1 oz white crème de menthe

½ oz cinnamon schnapps

1 scoop vanilla ice cream

Garnish:

cinnamon stick

sprig of mint

COOL CHERRY FREEZE

Combine all the ingredients in a blender with crushed ice, and blend until smooth. Pour into sour glasses, and garnish each with a maraschino cherry. Serves 2.

1 oz peppermint schnapps

1½ oz cherry brandy

1½ oz white crème de cacao

1 scoop cherry-vanilla ice cream

4 oz crushed ice

Garnish:

maraschino cherries

285

THE DRUNKEN ELF

Rim a martini glass with colored sugar and ground cinnamon candies. Combine all ingredients in a blender, and blend until smooth. Pour into the rimmed glass, and decorate with a candy cane.

1½ oz cinnamon schnapps

1½ oz green crème de menthe

1 oz cream

8 oz crushed ice

Garnish:

2 tbsp colored sugar

10 cinnamon candies, ground

candy cane

HOT AND CREAMY

Combine all ingredients in a blender except the half-and-half, and blend until frothy. Add half-and-half, pour into a cocktail glass, and sprinkle ground cinnamon on top.

½ oz cinnamon schnapps

1 oz vodka

2 oz half-and-half

4 oz ice

Garnish:
ground cinnamon

SPICED FRUIT PUNCH SLUSH

Combine all ingredients in a blender, and blend until thick and slushy. Pour into goblets, and garnish each with an orange wheel. Serves 2.

1 oz cinnamon schnapps

1 oz whiskey

1 oz rum

1½ oz fruit punch

1½ oz orange juice

24 oz crushed ice

Garnish:

orange wheels

CREAMY CARROT CAKE

Combine all ingredients in a blender, and blend until smooth. Pour into a tall glass, and top with whipped cream. Garnish with carrot rosettes.

1 oz cinnamon schnapps

½ oz butterscotch schnapps

1 oz hazelnut liqueur

1 oz carrot juice

1 oz pineapple juice

1 scoop vanilla ice cream

Garnish:

whipped cream

carrot rosettes

OATMEAL COOKIE

Rim a martini glass with brown sugar. Combine all ingredients in a blender, and blend until smooth. Pour into the rimmed glass, and sprinkle ground cinnamon on top.

½ oz butterscotch schnapps

½ oz Irish cream liqueur

¼ oz vanilla cream liqueur

¼ oz cinnamon schnapps

Garnish:

2 tbsp brown sugar

ground cinnamon

GINGERBREAD MAN

Rim a martini glass with gingerbread sprinkles, and then combine all ingredients in a blender. Blend until smooth. Pour into the cookie-rimmed glass, and garnish with a dusting of ground ginger.

1½ oz ginger schnapps

1½ oz vanilla vodka

½ oz butterscotch schnapps

½ oz Baileys Irish Cream

2 tbsp vanilla ice cream

Garnish:

gingerbread sprinkles

ground ginger

GOLDEN STAR

Combine all ingredients in a blender, and
blend to the consistency of a milk shake.
Pour into a highball glass, and garnish with
a dusting of ground nutmeg.

1 oz vanilla schnapps

¾ oz amaretto

**2 scoops vanilla
ice cream**

Garnish:

ground nutmeg

ALTERNATE ROOT

Combine all ingredients in a blender, and blend until slushy. Pour into a chilled beer mug, and serve.

3 oz root beer schnapps

4 oz orange juice

16 oz crushed ice

STRAWBERRY DREAM

Combine schnapps, half-and-half, sugar, and crushed ice in a blender, and blend at a high speed. Add the strawberries, and blend for 10 seconds. Pour into a pilsner glass, and top with whipped cream and a sprig of mint.

1 oz strawberry schnapps

2 oz half-and-half

1½ tbsp sugar

2 strawberries

16 oz crushed ice

Garnish:

whipped cream

sprig of mint

ABOVE: Berries 'n' Cream. Brighten up your creamy frozen cocktails with the flavor of ripe summer berries.

BERRIES 'N' CREAM

Combine all ingredients in a blender, and blend until smooth. Divide contents between two double-cocktail glasses, and garnish each with fresh strawberries, blueberries, and black raspberries. Serves 2.

¾ oz wildberry schnapps

½ oz spiced rum

3 oz strawberry daiquiri mix

2 tbsp raspberry jam

2 oz heavy cream

16 oz crushed ice

Garnish:

fresh berries

BANANAS 'N' CREAM

Combine ice cream, milk, and frozen bananas in a blender, and blend until smooth. Add the schnapps, and blend for an additional 10 seconds. Pour into a parfait glass, and decorate with an elaborate garnish.

2 oz butterscotch schnapps

1 oz crème de bananes

2 scoops vanilla ice cream

8 oz whole milk

2 sliced bananas, frozen

4 oz crushed ice

ABOVE: Peach Melba Freeze. Peach schnapps is often made from fully ripe peaches and stones, which give it a strong, fresh flavor. This rich cocktail takes advantage of a classic combination of fruit and dairy.

PEACH MELBA FREEZE

Combine all ingredients in a blender, and blend until smooth. Pour into a tall glass, and garnish with a fresh peach wedge.

¾ oz peach schnapps

¾ oz black raspberry liqueur

¾ oz Frangelico hazelnut liqueur

1 scoop vanilla ice cream

¾ oz light cream

1 oz raspberry jam

Garnish:

fresh peach

BRANDIED PEACHES 'N' CREAM

Combine all ingredients in a blender, and blend until smooth. Pour into a parfait glass, and garnish with a fresh peach wedge.

¾ oz peach schnapps

½ oz peach brandy

1½ oz cream of coconut

1 scoop vanilla ice cream

8 oz crushed ice

Garnish:

fresh peach

PEACHES 'N' CREAM

Combine all ingredients in a blender, and blend until smooth. Pour into a tall glass, and top with whipped cream drizzled with caramel sauce. Complete the garnish with a fresh slice of peach.

2 oz peach schnapps

½ oz orange liqueur

1½ oz heavy cream

2 scoops vanilla ice cream

Garnish:

whipped cream

fresh peach

caramel sauce

PLUMMY TONES

Combine all ingredients in a blender, and blend briefly at a low speed. Pour into a collins glass, and garnish with fresh plum.

2 oz plum schnapps

2 oz peach vodka

6 oz orange juice

1 tbsp condensed milk

4 oz crushed ice

Garnish:

fresh plum

FROZEN COCONUT

Combine all the ingredients in a blender, and blend until smooth. Pour into a highball glass, and garnish with a sprig of mint.

1 oz coconut schnapps

1½ oz white rum

3 tbsp coconut ice cream

4 oz crushed ice

Garnish:

sprig of mint

APPLE COLADA

Combine all the ingredients in a blender, and blend until smooth. Pour contents into a collins glass, and garnish with fresh apple.

2 oz apple schnapps

1 oz cream of coconut

1 oz half-and-half

16 oz crushed ice

Garnish:

fresh apple

FUZZY NAVEL SLUSH

In a large freezer container, combine water and sugar, and stir until the sugar is dissolved. Stir in the peach schnapps and orange juice and lemonade concentrates. Cover and freeze for at least four hours, occasionally stirring the mixture. When it is the consistency of Italian ice, scoop it into highball glasses about three-quarters of the way, and then top off with the lemon-lime soda. Stir, and then garnish each with an orange wedge. Serves 8 to 12.

8 oz peach schnapps

6 oz frozen orange juice concentrate

6 oz frozen lemonade concentrate

24 oz water

6–12 tbsp sugar

32 oz lemon-lime soda

Garnish:

orange wedges

ORANGE SHERBET SLUSH (page 310)

MOCKTAILS & SMOOTHIE

COCKTAILS

It's easy to think of cocktails only in terms of alcohol, but the same mixological principles that govern alcoholic drinks can be adapted for nonalcoholic drinks. The result can be a refreshing summer treat, especially with frozen beverages. If you keep in mind the first half of the classic cocktail formula—"one of sour, two of sweet, three of strong, four of weak"—you can concoct any number of delicious combinations of juice, fruit, herbs, syrups, and ice. So-called virgin daiquiris and margaritas are mainstays for people who want to enjoy a poolside bar or cozy indoor pub without indulging in alcohol. The benefits of these drinks extend beyond their taste and temperature: alcohol is a powerful diuretic, so leaving it out of drinks on a hot summer day means that you can enjoy all the refreshment of a frozen cocktail without the dehydration that would otherwise be part of the bargain. Also, kids love slushy drinks, so mocktails can be fun for everyone at a warm-weather gathering.

COCO COLADA

Combine all ingredients in a blender, and blend until smooth. Pour into a hurricane glass, and garnish extravagantly.

7 oz pineapple juice

2 oz cream of coconut

8 oz crushed ice

STRAWBERRY MOCKARITA

Rim margarita glasses with coarse salt, and then combine all ingredients in a blender. Blend at high speed until slushy. Pour into the salt-rimmed glasses, and garnish each with a lemon wheel and a fresh strawberry. Serves 6 to 8.

20 strawberries

4 oz fresh-squeezed lime juice

2 tbsp sugar

16 oz water

16 oz crushed ice

Garnish:

coarse salt

fresh strawberries

lemon wheels

ABOVE: Strawberry Mockarita. Most of the traditional frozen cocktails, such as margaritas, daiquiris, and the Piña Colada, easily translate into nonalcoholic "virgin" variations without losing flavor.

VIRGIN STRAWBERRY DAIQUIRI

Combine all ingredients in a blender, and blend until smooth. Pour into a martini glass, and garnish with a strawberry.

1 oz fresh lime juice

3 oz fresh strawberries

¼ tsp vanilla extract

1 tsp sugar

4 oz crushed ice

Garnish:

fresh strawberry

UNFORBIDDEN FRUIT

Chop the fruit into small pieces, and then combine all ingredients in a blender. Blend, pulsing the machine if necessary, until smooth. Pour into hurricane glasses, and garnish extravagantly. Serves 2.

4 oz frozen papaya

4 oz frozen pineapple

4 oz frozen mango

16 oz soy milk

1 tbsp honey

¼ tsp vanilla extract

4 oz crushed ice

COCO-KIWI

Reserving two slices of kiwi for the garnish, combine all ingredients in a blender, and blend until smooth. Pour into a martini glass, and garnish with the reserved kiwi.

1 kiwi, peeled
  and chopped

2 oz coconut milk

2 oz pineapple juice

2 tbsp cream of coconut

4 oz crushed ice

LIME BLITZ

Combine all ingredients in a blender, and blend until slushy. Pour into margarita glasses, and decorate each with a flamboyant garnish. Serves 2.

6 oz frozen limeade concentrate

3 oz pineapple juice

1 oz lemon juice

3 oz water

8 oz crushed ice

CITRUS SUNSHINE

Combine all ingredients in a blender, and blend until slushy. Pour into highball glasses, and garnish each with an orange wedge and a maraschino cherry. Serves 2.

4 scoops lemon sherbet

8 oz orange juice

4 oz grapefruit juice

2 oz honey

8 oz crushed ice

Garnish:

orange wedges

maraschino cherries

SHERBET SLUSH

Using the sherbet flavor of your choice, combine all ingredients in a blender, and blend until smooth. Pour into bolo grande glasses, top with whipped cream, and finish them with a fanciful garnish. Serves 4.

4 scoops sherbet (any flavor)

16 oz pineapple juice

16 oz orange juice

LEFT: Strawberry Sherbet Slush. This easy recipe is so versatile—just use your favorite sherbet flavor, and you have a new mocktail. You can also include fruit-flavored liqueurs or add rum or vodka for alcoholic versions.

BELOW: Orange Sherbet Slush. Dress up mocktails as you would any frozen cocktail with pretty fruit garnishes, such as orange wedges and maraschino cherries.

RASPBERRY FIZZLER

Combine raspberry juice and sherbet in
a blender, and blend until smooth. Pour
mixture into a hurricane glass, fill with club
soda, and stir. Garnish with fresh raspberries
and strawberries.

12 oz raspberry juice

3 scoops raspberry
   sherbet

4 oz club soda

Garnish:

fresh berries

MERRY BERRY

Reserving a few berries for the garnish, combine all ingredients in a blender, and blend until smooth. Pour into a tall glass, and garnish with the reserved berries.

2 oz fresh raspberries

2 oz fresh black currants

2 oz fresh strawberries

2 scoops vanilla ice cream

4 oz milk

PRETTY IN PINK

Combine all ingredients in a blender, and blend until smooth. Pour into tall glasses, and garnish each with a fresh strawberry. Serves 2.

4 oz fresh-squeezed orange juice

1 frozen banana

16 oz frozen strawberries

8 oz milk

4 oz vanilla yogurt

1–2 tbsp honey

Garnish:

fresh strawberries

COCONUT BASIL

Combine all ingredients in a cocktail shaker, and shake vigorously to release the flavor of the basil. Strain into a martini glass, and garnish with a sprig of basil.

2 oz cream of coconut

1 oz fresh pineapple juice

3 whole, fresh basil leaves

2 tbsp heavy cream

4 oz crushed ice

Garnish:

sprig of fresh basil

MOCHA SLIDE

Combine all ingredients except the chocolate syrup and heavy cream in a blender, and briefly blend. Add the heavy cream, and blend until well mixed. Drizzle the chocolate syrup down the inside of four wine glasses, and pour mixture inside. Top each with whipped cream, and garnish as simply or as extravagantly as you desire. Serves 4.

4 oz cold coffee

1 tsp hazelnut syrup

2 oz chocolate syrup

8 scoops vanilla ice cream

16 oz milk

12 oz heavy cream

Garnish:

whipped cream

INDEX

PHOTO CREDITS

Backgrounds by Number1411/Shutterstock.com
2–3 Leonid and Anna Dedukh/Shutterstock.com • 4 Elena
Elisseeva/Shutterstock.com • 5 ecadphoto/Shutterstock.com
• 6–7 Noam Wind/Shutterstock.com • 8 Kamira/Shutterstock.
com • 11 likedat/Shutterstock.com • 12 Vibe Images/
Shutterstock.com • 14 Tatiana Mihaliova/Shutterstock.
com • 15 Kzenon/Shutterstock.com • 16 Evgeny Karandaev/
Shutterstock.com • 17 Gina Stef/Shutterstock.com • 18–19
bellenixe/Shutterstock.com • 20 left Palmer Kane LLC/
Shutterstock.com • 20 right Danielle Boynton/Shutterstock.
com • 21 Shaiith/Shutterstock.com

Section One
22 Mariyana M/Shutterstock.com • 24 top Chiyacat/
Shutterstock.com • 24 bottom Monika Olszewska/
Shutterstock.com • 25 Elena Shashkina/Shutterstock.
com • 26 Markus Mainka/Shutterstock.com • 27 Shaiith/
Shutterstock.com • 28 gosphotodesign/Shutterstock.com
• 29 top Carlos Amarillo/Shutterstock.com • 29 bottom
Alliance/Shutterstock.com • 30 top Galene/Shutterstock.
com • 30 bottom Alessandro DYD/Shutterstock.com • 31
Lesya Dolyuk/Shutterstock.com • 32 verca/Shutterstock.
com • 33 Denis Tabler/Shutterstock.com • 34 top
Ruslan Olinchuk/Dreamstime.com • 34 bottom Kamira/
Shutterstock.com • 35 rmnoa357/Shutterstock.com • 36
Mariyana M/Shutterstock.com • 37 Wollertz/Shutterstock.
com • 38 top Dream79/Shutterstock.com • 38 bottom
Bochkarev Photography/Shutterstock.com • 39 sanneberg/
Shutterstock.com • 40 Africa Studio/Shutterstock.com •
41 Dmitry Lobanov/Shutterstock.com • 42 TheLionRoar/
Shutterstock.com • 43 top Anna Breitenberger/Shutterstock.
com • 43 bottom wavebreakmedia/Shutterstock.com
• 44 Bochkarev Photography/Shutterstock.com • 45
Bochkarev Photography/Shutterstock.com • 46 top REDAV/
Shutterstock.com • 46 bottom Ildi Papp/Shutterstock.
com • 47 funkyfrogstock/Shutterstock.com • 48 vsl/
Shutterstock.com • 49 Wiktory/Shutterstock.com • 50
Wollertz/Shutterstock.com • 51 top Wollertz/Shutterstock.
com • 51 bottom Markus Mainka/Shutterstock.com • 52
Wollertz/Shutterstock.com • 53 Bochkarev Photography/
Shutterstock.com • 54 funkyfrogstock/Shutterstock.com • 55
Ignia Andrei/Shutterstock.com • 56 Taratorki/Shutterstock.
com • 57 Andrew Grant/Dreamstime.com • 58 AnjelikaGr/
Shutterstock.com • 59 Olinchuk/Shutterstock.com • 60
gosphotodesign/Shutterstock.com • 61 top haveseen/
Shutterstock.com • 61 bottom haveseen/Shutterstock.com
• 62 Shebeko/Shutterstock.com • 63 Petr Jilek/Shutterstock.
com • 64 Bochkarev Photography/Shutterstock.com • 66
sutsaiy/Shutterstock.com • 67 Wollertz/Shutterstock.com
• 68 Ekaterina Bratova/Shutterstock.com • 69 kaband/
Shutterstock.com • 70 sutsaiy/Shutterstock.com • 71 Bogdan
Hoda/Dreamstime.com • 73 Igor Klimov/Shutterstock.com
• 74 graphia/Shutterstock.com • 75 Elena Shashkina/
Shutterstock.com • 76 Kovnir Andrii/Shutterstock.com • 77
Kovnir Andrii/Shutterstock.com • 78 mates/Shutterstock.com •
79 Lorraine Kourafas/Shutterstock.com • 80 svry/Shutterstock.
com • 81 stockcreations/Shutterstock.com • 82 Wollertz/

Shutterstock.com • 83 graphia/Shutterstock.com • 84
verchik/Shutterstock.com • 85 AnjelikaGr/Shutterstock.com •
86 Wollertz/Shutterstock.com • 87 Soultkd/Shutterstock.com
• 88 Natasha Breen/Shutterstock.com • 89 Stephanie Frey/
Shutterstock.com • 90 TheLionRoar/Shutterstock.com • 91
Tuullaa/Shutterstock.com • 92 Wollertz/Shutterstock.com •
93 Wollertz/Shutterstock.com • 94 Kovnir Andrii/Shutterstock.
com • 95 Miha Perosa/Shutterstock.com • 96 Galene/
Shutterstock.com • 97 Volodymyr Goinyk/Shutterstock.com

Section Two
98 Wollertz/Shutterstock.com • 100 Dustin Dennis/
Shutterstock.com • 101 Scruggelgreen/Shutterstock.
com • 102 Ultrashock/Shutterstock.com • 103 Kasia/
Shutterstock.com • 104 Vahan Abrahamyan/Shutterstock.com
• 105 Andrey Bashlykov/Shutterstock.com • 106 Wollertz/
Shutterstock.com • 107 Bochkarev Photography/Shutterstock.
com • 108 Wollertz/Shutterstock.com • 109 JM Travel
Photography/Shutterstock.com • 110 Wollertz/Shutterstock.
com • 111 Mark Skalny/Shutterstock.com • 112 Yauhen
Buzuk/Shutterstock.com • 113 Africa Studio/Shutterstock.com
• 114 vbmark/Shutterstock.com • 115 Wollertz/Shutterstock.
com • 116 Kondor83/Shutterstock.com • 117 Wollertz/
Shutterstock.com • 118 catlook/Shutterstock.com • 119
Letizia Spanò/Shutterstock.com • 120 mates/Shutterstock.
com • 121 REDAV/Shutterstock.com • 122 graphia/
Shutterstock.com • 123 Wollertz/Shutterstock.com • 124
svry/Shutterstock.com • 125 Agnes Kantaruk/Shutterstock.
com • 126 Otokimus/Shutterstock.com • 127 IngridHS/
Shutterstock.com • 128 Africa Studio/Shutterstock.com • 129
Yauhen Buzuk/Shutterstock.com • 131 Wollertz/Shutterstock.
com • 132 Greg Nesbit Photography/Shutterstock.com • 133
Wollertz/Shutterstock.com • 134 Elena Ray/Shutterstock.com
• 135 top withGod/Shutterstock.com • 135 bottom Mariyana
M/Shutterstock.com • 136 Marut Prasertsri/Shutterstock.
com • 137 Tyler Olson/Shutterstock.com • 138 photopixel/
Shutterstock.com • 139 Evgeny Karandaev/Shutterstock.
com • 140 Wollertz/Shutterstock.com • 141 Avatar_023/
Shutterstock.com • 142 ARENA Creative/Shutterstock.com •
143 Petr Jilek/Shutterstock.com • 145 Olinchuk/Shutterstock.
com • 146 Elena Ray/Shutterstock.com • 147 186PIX/
Shutterstock.com • 148 Shebeko/Shutterstock.com • 149
sutsaiy/Shutterstock.com

Section Three
150 Volodymyr Goinyk/Shutterstock.com • 152 Wollertz/
Shutterstock.com • 153 GRAFVISION/Dreamstime.com •
154 VictorH11/Shutterstock.com • 155 top Deymos.HR/
Shutterstock.com • 155 bottom Zaichenko Olga/Shutterstock.
com • 156 Quinn Martin/Shutterstock.com • 157 Pinkyone/
Shutterstock.com • 158 Yarygin/Shutterstock.com • 159
Maxisport/Shutterstock.com • 160 Jelly/Shutterstock.com
• 161 svetlovskiy/Shutterstock.com • 162 Peredniankina/
Shutterstock.com • 163 Kasia/Shutterstock.com • 164
Africa Studio/Shutterstock.com • 165 Wollertz/Shutterstock.
com • 166 Wollertz/Shutterstock.com • 167 Juraj Rasla/
Shutterstock.com • 168 svry/Shutterstock.com • 169 Africa

Studio/Shutterstock.com • 170 jabiru/Shutterstock.com • 171 Volha Harchychka/Dreamstime.com • 172 Elizaveta Shagliy/Shutterstock.com • 173 Ricardo Villasenor/Shutterstock.com • 174 top Dream79/Shutterstock.com • 174 bottom Gamzova Olga/Shutterstock.com • 175 Ramon L. Farinos/Shutterstock.com • 176 sutsaiy/Shutterstock.com • 177 Luiz Rocha/Shutterstock.com • 178 Everything/Shutterstock.com • 180 Kasia/Shutterstock.com • 181 Denis Tabler/Shutterstock.com • 182 patronestaff/Shutterstock.com • 183 Bochkarev Photography/Shutterstock.com • 184 Vitaliy Netiaga/Shutterstock.com • 185 RGB Digital/Philippa Baile • 186 Zadorozhnyi Viktor/Shutterstock.com • 187 Wollertz/Shutterstock.com • 188 Settawat Udom/Shutterstock.com • 189 Vitalfoto/Shutterstock.com • 190 svry/Shutterstock.com • 191 Free-lance/Shutterstock.com • 193 Lostry7/Shutterstock.com • 194 Viktorfischer/Dreamstime.com • 195 stocknadia/Shutterstock.com • 196 Peredniankina/Shutterstock.com • 197 Wollertz/Dreamstime.com • 199 Steve Allen/Shutterstock.com • 200 Iura_Atom/Shutterstock.com • 201 Letizia Spanò/Shutterstock.com • 202 Elzbieta Sekowska/Shutterstock.com • 202 Palmer Kane LLC/Shutterstock.com • 203 vbmark/Shutterstock.com • 204 Africa Studio/Shutterstock.com • 205 Visionsi/Shutterstock.com • 206 Lost Mountain Studio/Shutterstock.com • 208 Volodymyr Goinyk/Shutterstock.com • 209 Elena Elisseeva/Shutterstock.com • 210 Lisovskaya Natalia/Shutterstock.com • 211 Slawomir Fajer/Shutterstock.com • 212 Greg Nesbit Photography/Shutterstock.com • 213 Wollertz/Shutterstock.com • 214 Galene/Shutterstock.com • 215 Sanne Berg/Dreamstime.com • 216 Andreas Argirakis/Shutterstock.com • 217 BARRI/Shutterstock.com • 218 NADKI/Shutterstock.com • 219 Irafael/Shutterstock.com • 220 Joyce Marrero/Shutterstock.com • 221 Barbara Neveu/Shutterstock.com • 222 Shebeko/Shutterstock.com • 223 Sisacorn/Shutterstock.com

Section Four

224 Carlos Rondon/Shutterstock.com • 226 Africa Studio/Shutterstock.com • 227 svry/Shutterstock.com • 228 top Dusan002/Shutterstock.com • 228 bottom RGB Digital/Jeremy Baile • 229 Letizia Spanò/Shutterstock.com • 230 Carlos Rondon/Shutterstock.com • 231 Netfalls - Remy Musser/Shutterstock.com • 232 Worachat Sodsri/Shutterstock.com • 233 Robcartorres/Shutterstock.com • 234 svry/Shutterstock.com • 235 top svry/Shutterstock.com • 235 bottom Vasin Lee/Shutterstock.com • 236 Vahan Abrahamyan/Shutterstock.com • 237 Ildi Papp/Shutterstock.com • 238 Dmitry Fischer/Shutterstock.com • 239 sarsmis/Shutterstock.com • 240 Wollertz/Shutterstock.com • 241 vsl/Shutterstock.com • 242 REDAV/Shutterstock.com • 243 Brent Hofacker/Shutterstock.com • 244 aliasemma/Shutterstock.com • 245 Jelly/Shutterstock.com • 246 RGB Digital/Philippa Baile • 247 Andreas Argirakis/Shutterstock.com • 248 tiverylucky/Shutterstock.com • 249 Ramona D'viola/Dreamstime.com • 250 RGB Digital/Jeremy Baile • 251 RGB Digital/Philippa Baile • 252 Andreas Argirakis/Shutterstock.com • 253 Lena Ivanova/Shutterstock.com • 254 White Room/Shutterstock.com • 255 svry/Shutterstock.com

Section Five

256 Scruggelgreen/Shutterstock.com • 258 top Scruggelgreen/Shutterstock.com • 258 bottom Stockfotocz/Dreamstime.com • 259 Cameron Whitman/Shutterstock.com • 260 Jelly/Shutterstock.com • 261 Eduard Zhukov/Shutterstock.com • 263 Dallas Events Inc/Shutterstock.com • 264 John Wollwerth/Shutterstock.com • 265 Scruggelgreen/Shutterstock.com • 266 Palmer Kane LLC/Shutterstock.com • 267 Leigh Anne Meeks/Shutterstock.com • 268 top 3523studio/Shutterstock.com • 268 bottom 3523studio/Shutterstock.com • 269 3523studio/Shutterstock.com • 270 Bochkarev Photography/Shutterstock.com • 271 dias46/Shutterstock.com • 272 top Lschirmbeck/Dreamstime.com • 272 bottom grafvision/Shutterstock.com • 273 dashkin14/Shutterstock.com • 274 Mark Skalny/Dreamstime.com • 275 Ognjen Maravic/Dreamstime.com • 276 Bochkarev Photography/Shutterstock.com • 277 GVictoria/Shutterstock.com • 278 Surrphoto/Shutterstock.com • 279 Africa Studio/Shutterstock.com

Section Six

280 Worachat Sodsri/Shutterstock.com • 282 Wiktory/Shutterstock.com • 283 pixelliebe/Shutterstock.com • 284 tulpahn/Shutterstock.com • 285 Worachat Sodsri/Shutterstock.com • 286 Michael C. Gray/Shutterstock.com • 287 REDAV/Shutterstock.com • 288 Worachat Sodsri/Shutterstock.com • 289 deuxmilledeux/Shutterstock.com • 290 Foodio/Shutterstock.com • 291 Michael C. Gray/Shutterstock.com • 292 Aivolie/Shutterstock.com • 293 bochimsang12/Shutterstock.com • 294 Piyato/Shutterstock.com • 295 Andrei Levitskiy/Dreamstime.com • 296 Lecic/Shutterstock.com • 297 Arina P Habich/Shutterstock.com • 298 Volodymyr Goinyk/Shutterstock.com • 299 Galene/Shutterstock.com • 300 Deymos.HR/Shutterstock.com • 301 Barbara Neveu/Shutterstock.com

Section Seven

302 Larry St. Pierre/Shutterstock.com • 304 REDAV/Shutterstock.com • 305 alexsmaga/Shutterstock.com • 306 Gina Stef/Shutterstock.com • 307 Boris Ryzhkov/Dreamstime.com • 308 Lena Ivanova/Shutterstock.com • 309 R. Gino Santa Maria / Shutterfree, LLC/Dreamstime.com • 310 top Larry St. Pierre/Shutterstock.com • 310 bottom Larry St. Pierre/Shutterstock.com • 311 Gina Stef/Shutterstock.com • 312 skostrez/Shutterstock.com • 313 Letizia Spanò/Shutterstock.com • 314 Kuleczka/Dreamstime.com • 315 Shebeko/Shutterstock.com